SHORT CUTS

INTRODUCTIONS TO FILM STUDIES

SPECTATORSHIP

THE POWER OF LOOKING ON

MICHELE AARON

WALLFLOWER

LONDON and NEW YORK

A Wallflower Paperback

First published in Great Britain in 2007 by
Wallflower Press
6a Middleton Place, Langham Street, London, W1W 7TE
www.wallflowerpress.co.uk

A catalogue record for this book is available from the British Library

ISBN 978 1 905674 01 5

Book design by Rob Bowden Design

Printed in Great Britain by Antony Rowe Ltd, Chippenham, Wiltshire

CONTENTS

ACKNOWLEDGEMENTS

First thanks go to Yoram Allon for his enthusiasm and patience: you're a mensch. For invaluable feedback on various chapters, I am grateful to Jean Aaron, Tanya Krzywinska, Scott Lucas, Monica Pearl and Julianne Pidduck, but especially to Catherine Grant without whose insight and generosity this project would not have been completed. Some of this book's discussions began during my doctoral research in the mid-1990s at the University of Southampton. My appreciation goes to my PhD supervisor Linda Ruth Williams, who I would also like to thank for providing me with the introduction to her book on the Erotic Thriller film in advance of its publication. Chapter Four's discussion, 'Self-reflexivity and the complicitous spectator', was first published within *The Spectacle of the Real: From Hollywood to Reality TV and Beyond*, edited by Geoff King (2005).

This book is dedicated with love and gratitude to my parents
Jean and Martin Aaron

INTRODUCTION

This book traces a history of spectatorship studies. It is a history that contains various, and often competing, descriptions of what happens to the individual in the cinema, what characterises his or her engagement and what accounts for his or her interpretation of a film. As such, spectatorship represents a site of conflict between methodologies: the battle between, say, the unconscious processes of psychoanalysis, or the social processes of cultural studies, to best explain the spectator's experience. Within these various versions of spectatorship, what remains central is the question of the spectator's agency: the individual's *own* role and activity in participating in the pleasures of the text, in determining the meaning of a film and, even, the meaningfulness of cinema. The discussion of spectatorship has always been bound up with this question in its negotiation of the spectator's activity or passivity, manipulation or resistance, distance or implication. It is this that maintains spectatorship as a crucial issue within critical thinking in general and film studies in particular. It is the aim of this book to retell the discussion of spectatorship as a story of agency, which in paring down methodological and other tensions prioritises the spectator's response and responsibility.

Seeing spectatorship as a site of conflict is hardly new. Fundamental to an understanding of what a spectator is, is to note what it is not – that is, that a spectator is not a viewer. The viewer, according to cultural studies, is the live, breathing, actual audience member, coming from a specific socio-historical context. This viewer exists in sharp contrast to the spectator as 'subject', a product of the ideological machinations of cinema, of 1970s' film theory's classical model of spectatorship. One could argue that bridging the seeming chasm between the spectator and the viewer represents the terrain of spectatorship studies. This is certainly how its major interpreters have seen it. For Judith Mayne, whose *Cinema and Spectatorship* is the key book on the subject, spectatorship studies is bent on the 'complicated negotiations' between these polarised positions (1993: 9). Similarly, when Janet Staiger privileged 'context-activated models' (1992: 59) she was not simply arguing for the synthetic approach to spectatorship, but deliberately uniting the often exclusive focuses upon text, or reader, or social formation. *Spectatorship: The Power of Looking On* similarly seeks to reconcile the previously conflicted elements, to privilege synthesis. In this way, not only will we explore the interaction of textual practices, psychological processes and social context in the first half of the book but, in the film analyses of the second half, we will put this triangulation into practice.

Retaining the 'spectator' as our principal player, however, is not meant to dismiss the viewer or cultural studies, far from it. Unlike its supposed usurpers – especially the viewer as 'decoder' – the spectator can sustain the interplay of unconscious desires, social influences and textual provocations, as will be shown. But retaining the spectator also points to the influence upon this book of reader-response theory (a body of criticism whose main inheritor was, in fact, cultural studies). Reader-response theory argues that something particular happens when we read, that the 'self' of the reader becomes entangled, encompassed or even lost within the 'self' of the text. Involving critics from various schools of thought – formalists, phenomenologists, structuralists, psychoanalysts – the experience of reading was seen to cause the self to undergo some kind of transformation. George Poulet saw it as an inhabitation by another (1969: 55), Stanley Fish refers to a disappearance (1980: 335), Jonathan Culler to a dissolution (1975: 28) and Roland Barthes to a kind of 'ecstatic loss' (1981: 32). For Wolfgang Iser (1974) the self merges with the text, for Norman Holland (1980) it is effaced and for Wayne Booth (1988) it is occupied by the text.

As well as refocusing attention upon the reader, all these theorists – though they had their different critical agendas – undermined the distinction between the subject (reader) and object (text), a distinction or distance that the reader is at pains to sustain. It is within this disintegration of the distance or insulation from the text of the reader or, here, the spectator, that this book is located. This is why I place such emphasis upon textual analysis: for the spectator's submersion in and submission to the text (to whatever degree) must be understood as an inevitable part of the act of engagement. Though textual analysis, as we shall see, exposes the spectator's various claims to a distance from the text, it is not enough to explain the *need* for this distance. For this we must turn to psychoanalysis which offers us various paradigms for understanding such a need in terms of the unconscious anxieties and desires that the text provokes. And disavowal will prove a primary method for managing the tension between these two. But this tension can only be thoroughly understood through reference to the social sphere as well and its imposition of the mores and morals that govern or at least guide our public behaviours. Rather than delineate, then, the various routes on from the classical model – empiricism, cognitivism, historicism, among others – as narratives of spectatorship studies have so productively done already (see, for example, Staiger 1992, Mayne 1993, Cook 1999), this book, instead, promotes a counter-model of spectatorship that locates the spectator's submission within an interaction of textual, social and psychic processes. Crucially, it also updates debates on the spectator through the contemporary context of the sexualisation of cinema, the proliferation and convergence of screen media and the cultural 'turn to ethics'. Pitting the spectator's submission against complicity, fantasy against prurience, impartiality against accountability, *Spectatorship: The Power of Looking On* will provide a new look at a relatively old subject for film studies.

The 'looking on', then, of spectatorship points to not only the spectator's suspect claim to neutrality through his or her bid to distance but the privilege that such a claim represents. When Mary Ann Doane suggested that women 'would seem to be perfect spectators, culturally positioned as they are outside the arena of history, politics, production – "looking on"' (1987: 2), she was noting the exclusionary measures of cinema and of film theory, which kept woman in her place, rather than the social (or psychic) benefits of a vantage point. Of course, women are not the only 'others' to be detached from cultural representation. Indeed, as E. Ann Kaplan suggests, it is not the male gaze or the female gaze of spectatorship that must preoccupy us, but the imperial gaze (1995: 180). So while this book traces a history of spectatorship studies, it is not only a particular history that is being traced but the dominant one. Placing the birth of the spectator within the social context of post-'68 France, as I do in chapter one, means for me that spectatorship's formative years are thoroughly Eurocentric. When we step on from this crucial period of critical theory towards the Anglo-American axis of cine-psychoanalysis, feminist criticism and cultural studies, we continue to stage spectatorship theory within the coordinates of the Western Academy. These coordinates provide one obvious stage for the story, but it is one that has been much criticised within, for example, discussions of Third Cinema (see, for example, Guneratne & Dissanayake 2003). It is not the aim of this book to take on, or do justice to, the 'otherised' (Kaplan 1995: 179) within film and spectatorship, but this is far from a de-politicised study. Indeed, this book argues that there is much at stake – socially and, finally, ethically – in continuing to challenge and re-interpret the dominant frameworks from within. As such, it both revisits the classics of Hollywood and explores films from beyond the common frame of dominant cinema, such as examples from the Danish film movement, Dogme 95.

The aim of this book, then, is to retell the discussion of spectatorship as a story of agency, which prioritises the spectator's response and responsibility to reveal spectatorship as an intrinsically politicised subject. In the chapters that follow we will visit and redirect the key issues in the emergence of spectatorship theory through the lens of this intention. Where chapter one will reveal the original conception of the spectator as a powerless and passive product of the ideological institution of cinema, chapter two asks how the difference between spectators, in particular sexual difference, determines our understanding of their agency, especially their relationship to passivity. Chapter three goes on to dismantle the previous chapters' sadistic model of the pleasures of spectatorship, to suggest instead their masochism. As masochistic, the spectator's visual and other pleasures will be found to be grounded in the 'unpleasures' offered by film. As masochistic, the spectator's experience will be shown to be consensual and contractual and the submission that characterises spectatorship to embody, rather than expel, agency. In chapter four we ask whether there are any consequences of the spectator's complicity. Framing contemporary spectatorship in the proliferation of socially or emotionally problematic images, the book ends with a call for an ethical reconsideration of the spectator's experience.

1   THE BIRTH OF THE SPECTATOR

The origins of spectatorship as a topic of debate are to be situated within two rather dramatic (and not unrelated) developments that took place within French social history on the one hand, and within critical theory on the other. The first was the wave of political protests centred on Paris in May 1968 and around the country over the next month or two. The second, and more significant for our purposes, was Structuralism, an analytical approach and practice that came to prominence in the 1960s and 1970s. The connections between the two are variously under- and over-estimated, but what is unshakeable is that both represented a profound reappraisal of individual agency.[1] The impact of this reappraisal upon film theory would result in the birth (and death) of the spectator.

In May 1968, major student protests combined with extensive strike action to leave France temporarily 'paralysed with more than eight million workers on strike, no public transport and precious little petrol' (Reader 1993: 14). What was remarkable about these events was not only their scale but their apparent uniting of students, workers and intellectuals in a rarely seen utopian spirit of revolution.[2] Sylvia Harvey sees these events as an 'impetus' to the burgeoning discussions of ideology in general and the potential of radical filmmaking in particular (1980: 45). They must certainly be seen as a trigger to the production of radical theory; thereafter writings on film were to become preoccupied with its political nature and effects and the importance of theory for understanding and harnessing its potential. Most of this radical theory would be located, sometimes retroactively, under the banner of Structuralism. Before exploring structuralist film theory, it would be extremely helpful to offer a brief illumination of what Structuralism is.

What is Structuralism?

'Any old rubbish erected into a system' (May '68 graffiti; Bernard 1989)

We humans are constantly making meaning out of the things that we encounter. We are constantly interpreting our world through its most blatant or more abstract messages (the difference, say, between the threatening words 'I'm warning you' and a severed horse head in your bed). We do not just read words, but symbols, faces, the sky. Information gets conveyed, or encoded, in numerous ways. For example: I know my friend is sad because i) she told me so, ii) she is crying, iii) her floor is scattered with soggy hankies, iv) her flatmate concurs. Things that mean, otherwise known as 'signs' (in this case: tears, soggy hankies, concerned flatmate), are everywhere. But how do they gain meaning? Firstly, it is a question of specificity, of difference: a soggy tea towel would not suggest that my friend had been crying but that she has done the washing up. Secondly it is a question of context: a soggy hanky spilling out of a cracked ceiling suggests that there is a leak and has nothing to do with my poor friend and her problems.[3] So, meaning is made through a sign's difference from other signs and through context. This is all to say that meaning is relational, it is a system based on relationships (in this case between 'soggy hanky' and 'soggy tea towel' but equally between 'soggy hanky' and 'sad friend'). These relationships are governed by our convention-determined understanding of difference and context, an understanding that operates as a set of laws or codes. These conventions, laws or codes dictate how we read the signs – never in isolation – and in this sense meaning/language must be seen as being pre-structured.

This very basic foray into the extremely important semiotic theory of Swiss linguist Ferdinand de Saussure is crucial to our comprehension of Structuralism, for Structuralism was its application to objects and activities other than language (de Saussure 1966). The project of Structuralism was to reveal everything – from kinship systems (Claude Levi-Strauss) to cultural myths (Roland Barthes) to the human psyche (Jacques Lacan) – as functioning like language, like a system of related signs governed by laws or codes. Nothing has meaning in itself, essentially, but only through its underlying relationship with all other things translated through convention. It is these structural relationships, this pre-structure, that are all important.

Structuralism is thus based, in the first instance, in the realisation that if human actions and productions have a meaning there must be an underlying system of distinctions and conventions which makes meaning possible (Culler 1975: 4).

What does Structuralism have to do with film?

There are many ways in which Structuralism impacted upon film theory: film was scrutinised as a language, its underlying structure (the meaning-determining relationships between narrative and genre say, or camera-angles and costume or even between one shot and another) became, and remains, a major focus of attention (and we will come to this later). But what is important for now is that structuralist film theory would come to emphasise the pre-structure of film and the conventional, or rather, ideologically pre-determined position of the spectator that it produces. The key starting point here is not with a film theorist but with Louis Althusser, a French Marxist theorist who would have a profound effect on film studies, and, in particular, on the birth of the spectator. His rethinking of Marxist notions of state control would instate the notion of the 'subject' into the functioning of ideology. When applied to cinema, this 'subject' would emerge as the hypothetical spectator of 1970s film theory.

Writing from the context of radical French thought in the wake of 1968, Althusser's main concern was with understanding and explaining how dominant, capitalist society managed to perpetuate its own disharmonious system. In his seminal essay 'Ideology and Ideological State Apparatuses: Notes towards an Investigation', first published in 1969, he offered a breakdown of society that would explain this conceit. Building upon the Marxist theory of the state as a repressive apparatus, Althusser re-categorised its components (government, army, police, prisons) as Repressive State Apparatuses (RSAs) which operate primarily through force. He then distinguished a further set of institutions, those from the private domain, which operate primarily through ideology. These he called Ideological State Apparatuses (ISAs) and included amongst them the church, family, trade unions and media (and by extension, can be added, the cinema). Despite the RSAs' formidable strength, it was the latter, the ISAs, that were held responsible for the main work of mass control through the more subtle but more insidious processes that they represented. Applying Lacan's psychoanalytic theories of (the pre-structure of) subject formation, specifically those articulated via the mirror stage, Althusser suggested that the ISAs create ideologically-governed subjectivity.

Althusser distinguishes a two-pronged process of subject formation taking place in ideology's acting through the ISAs: *interpellation* and *(mis)recognition*: 'Ideology Interpellates Individuals as Subjects … all ideology has the function (which defines it) of "constituting" concrete individuals as subjects' (1971: 170–1). An individual is interpellated – assigned a name, place and identity – by society's various institutions. This name, place and identity is accepted by the individual who cannot help but recognise him or herself in these prescriptions. Anthony Easthope offers the useful example of the amorphous child who can enter school at five or six 'and answer individually when the teacher calls out "his" name' (1993: 10). We are the sense of ourselves that others have and use in their interactions with us. We are the identity we have been ascribed, for example of teacher, nurse, hairdresser, mother, daughter, father. But we are also always more than these things, yet for the ease or convention of social existence we accept these prescriptions, we (mis)recognise ourselves as them, and thus the system – the pre-structure of subjectivity – reproduces itself. As Robert Lapsley and Michael Westlake put it:

> Individuals acquiesce in these identities and are precisely subjected to them. Ideology obtains from individuals the recognition that they really do occupy the place it designates as theirs. (1989: 8)

However, recognition is always, ultimately, grounded in misrecognition.[4] It is a process of ideology that represents an approximation, a generalisation, a vagueness received as accuracy. It represents, as Althusser so famously put it, individuals' *'imaginary relationship* … to their real conditions of existence'* (1971: 153). This system of subject formation hinges upon individuals' acceptance of a falsity: that they are, undoubtedly, what they have been interpellated as; that, crucially, they have exercised individuality and choice (that is, agency) in assuming this identity. Ideology, then, is the willing acceptance of things not really true, it is an embracing of illusion, and the illusion of agency. What better place, then, to explore ideology than in the home-ground of illusion: cinema.

Cinema as ideology

The challenge of film theory after the events of 1968 and the writings of Althusser, was to figure out how cinema worked ideologically to constitute the subject within a system of 'imagined relations', that depended upon the individual's illusion of agency to fuel its reproduction. Let us rephrase this as a series of more simple questions: How might cinema work to inter-pellate the subject? How might cinema set up the individual's 'imaginary relation' to reality (the illusion upon which [mis]recognition is based)? How might cinema provide the subject with an illusion of agency? Why does the system perpetuate itself; why do they keep producing and we keep watching films that replicate the unequal if not depraved society that we might otherwise oppose?

1970s film theory would offer answers to each of these but before attending them let us note the emerging emphasis upon illusion. What the questions rotate around and what is central to the discussion of ideology is the structure and appeal of illusion. It is no surprise then that psycho-analysis, as the theorisation of the individual's relation to illusion, to the imaginary, to fantasy, would gain in importance during this period. Indeed, what proved so inspiring about Althusser's work was the conjoining of the effects of material and social conditions with psychological ones. This union, so fundamental to ideology, would trigger the construction of a model of classical spectatorship, which, as psychoanalytic film theory, would become the cornerstone of 1970s film theory.

The immediate offspring of Althusser's work within film criticism was *apparatus theory*. As its name implies, it shared his approach by seeing cinema as an institution that depended upon the interaction between material conditions and social and psychic processes for its ideological stature. The film apparatus – the machinery or mechanism of cinema – is far more than just the camera/projector but instead represents the experience of film generated by the triangulation of projector, spectator and screen. It is the interplay of these three: of the technical (projection), the physical (seated spectator in darkened auditorium) and the psychic (the psychological effects of this configuration and of the film viewed). Apparatus theory, then, considered how the technical set up for showing the film, the practical/physical set up for watching the film and the psychological set up for engaging with it, interact to enact and perpetuate the ideological experience.

The first to write about cinema in Althusserian terms was Jean-Louis Baudry in his article, published in the French journal *Cinéthique* in 1970, 'Ideological Effects of the Basic Cinematographic Apparatus'. He, and Christian Metz even more so, was highly influential in explaining the spectator's 'imaginary relation' to the screen within the psychoanalytic terms of the infant's relationship to the mirror. While psychoanalysis will occupy us increasingly, I want first to distinguish three points made by Baudry which map out the affair between apparatus theory and the passive spectator, but also offer answers to those questions set at the start of this discussion of cinema as ideology.

Firstly, the spectator is seen as placed by the film apparatus in a supremely powerful and yet virtual position, as being transcendent. Borrowing from art theory, and in particular the work of Marcel Pleynet (1969), published in a previous issue of *Cinéthique*, Baudry invokes the 'monocular vision' and *quattrocentro* perspective of Italian Renaissance painting to demonstrate how the film image is constructed and unfolds for the all-seeing, all-powerful spectator. Replicating the 'ideology inherent in perspective' in these artworks, cinema is 'based on the principle of a fixed point of reference to which the visualised objects are organised, it specifies in return the position of the "subject", the very spot it must necessarily occupy ... It lays out the space of an ideal vision and in this way assures the necessity of a transcendence' (1985: 534). Like the classical composition of visual art, the film image is laid out in such a way as to channel the (anticipated) spectator's uni-directional view: the image is composed *for* the spectator's vision yet seems to be a product *of* the spectator's vision. The opening establishing shot from *A Fistful of Dollars* (1964) provides a perfect example of just this kind of visual composition in which the epic proportions of the landscape are generated for, and seemingly by, the spectator's gaze.

The spectator is born in the vanishing point generated by perspective, is summoned into hypothetical existence by the visual structure. What comes into being is the transcendent yet absent spectator – an illusion of agency indeed. As Veijo Hietala puts it: 'the *quattrocentro* positions the spectator as the target of its address at the same time, however, concealing this positioning by allowing the subject an illusory sense of him/herself as the producer of meaning' (1991: 74).

Secondly, Baudry asserts that despite being a 'moving image' that 'might permit ... a multiplicity of point of views', especially through editing (although, remember, it is not the text but the technical which concerns Baudry), cinema still sustains the 'monocular vision' of the camera and of the eye (1985: 534). It does this by effacing discontinuity through the illusion of sameness. Taking frames separately, film is revealed as constituted by the succession of miniscule but amounting differences between each frame. Projection allows these to be seen as a smooth, seamless whole: 'The projection mechanism allows the differential elements (the discontinuity inscribed by the camera) to be suppressed ... The individual images as such disappear so that movement and continuity can appear' (1985: 536). The crucial point, and one that will be taken up by numerous other writers on film and by me later, is that the spectator's experience relies upon some sort of denial. For Baudry it is a 'denial of difference' that feeds the film and furnishes the spectator with the welcomed illusion. Jean-Louis Comolli, another important name in apparatus theory, took this further. In 'Machines of the Visible' he extended this denial of difference to the early spectator's acceptance of the primitive film image's gross break with reality, its being 'devoid of colour, nuance, fluidity' (1980: 124). Comolli worked with stronger terms. Rather than illusion, Comolli offered the spectator's 'delusion', thereby suggesting his or her culpability in the 'imagined relations'. Similarly, his spectator more than denied difference, he/she *disavowed* it. In so doing his/her complicity in the process (albeit unconscious) was emphasised: 'the spectator is anyhow well aware of the artifice but he/she prefers all the same to believe in it' (1980: 133). In this way, the issue of the spectator's agency, the agency behind desire, behind complicity, lurks in the background. Cinema, for its part, worked with technical developments to perpetuate this disavowal; to keep the illusion/delusion compelling and the technology masked: 'the act of disavowal renewing the deception could continue to be accomplished "automatically", in a reflex manner, without any disturbance of the spectacle, above all without any work or effort on the part of the spectator' (ibid.).

The third important discussion to be drawn from Baudry's work introduces the significance of identification. Likening spectatorship to the mirror stage, Baudry establishes the reasons for the spectator's imaginary relation to the screen. But what is the mirror stage? According to Lacan, the mirror stage occurs during a baby's first six to eighteen months when, held up to a mirror by its mother, the baby distinguishes itself in the reflection. The image that it recognises, however, is a far more competent and complete self than our motor-skill-challenged baby, limbs-a-flailing, unable to recognise the limits of its body. Identification is, therefore, rooted in (mis)recognition. Cinema, for Baudry, repeats the conditions (privileged by Lacan) that trigger this scenario: the 'suspension of mobility and predominance of visual function' (1985: 539). It also, therefore, repeats the process's self-cohering function, its 'imaginary constitution of the self' both by 'unit[ing] the discontinuous fragments of phenomena, of lived experience, into unifying meaning' for the transcendental subject, and by invoking the spectator's identification with on-screen characters (1985: 540). While Baudry isolates two levels of identification here – one pertaining to the image itself, the other to the characters within the image – it is Metz who more fully (and more successfully) explained them.

In his article 'The Imaginary Signifier', first published in 1975, Metz prioritises this initial identification with the screen image as a resuscitation of the earlier experience of the mirror. Indeed, the mirror stage, that crucial event in ego formation – primary identification – provided Metz with the perfect paradigm for the spectator's experience in front of the cinema screen: his or her ability to identify with the on-screen figure. This identification with the screen-image can only occur because 'the spectator has already known the experience of the mirror (of the true mirror), and is thus able to constitute a world of objects without having first to recognise himself within it' (1982: 46). He called this reviving of that first encounter primary cinematic identification. In 'Story/Discourse' he clarifies its ideological weight, how it interpellates the subject and provides the illusion of agency. It is an identification 'with the (invisible) seeing agency of the film itself as discourse, as the agency which *puts forward* the story and shows it to us. Insofar as it abolishes all traces of the subject of the enunciation [for example, the projectionist], the traditional film succeeds in giving the spectator the impression that he is himself that subject' (1985: 548). Identifications with characters were secondary cinematic identifications, tertiary even. Thus, through Metz and primary cinematic identification, we receive the fuller weight of the cinema's construction of the ideological subject, the complete merging of camera and subjectivity. Metz's crucial contribution to film studies was this absolute given that film could not be discussed without reference to the unconscious and its various desire- or fantasy-fuelled expressions, like voyeurism and exhibitionism (there will be more on these later). As well as cementing the importance of the mirror stage within the emerging cine-psychoanalysis, Metz centralised other psychic processes of subject formation in the understanding of spectatorial engagement, most importantly the idea that cinema was *fetishistic*.

Freud's theory of fetishism (1991d) focused upon the burgeoning anxieties of the small child – that is the small male child – who has noticed that his mother has no penis and realised that he too could lose his or have it taken away. An almost unbearable thought, the child finds ways to pretend that this threat of castration does not exist. In place of the absent penis, he installs a fetish; he covers over the original lack with a cherished alternative. This illusory covering up of reality provided the basis for Metz to distinguish cinema as, similarly, a fetishistic process. He writes: 'Any spectator will tell you that he "doesn't believe it", but everything happens as if there were nonetheless someone to be deceived, someone who really would "believe in it"' (1982: 72). Cinema, according to Metz, covered over or made up for cinema's lack of reality through the heightened aesthetics, or over-valuation, of the image. The apparatus worked in such a way as to prevent the spectator from thinking about the absence of reality, it disavowed this loss. In calling cinema fetishistic, in positing spectatorship through disavowal, Metz rooted it in reassurance. 'Our' acceptance, then, of those 'imagined relations', becomes that much more understandable.

Apparatus theory traded on the acceptance of a hypothetical, generalised spectator as a product of the institution of cinema as manifested in the apparatus and its material, physical and psychological constructions. Countless voices would rise to challenge the theorists' universalising momentum (and we shall be hearing from many of them below) but its greatest reformer – for she supported rather than decried apparatus theory – was Laura Mulvey with her article 'Visual Pleasure and Narrative Cinema', first published in 1975. In this extremely influential piece, Mulvey demonstrated how gender impacted upon spectatorship, how the illusion, furnishing subjectivity, was tailored to and by sexual difference.[5]

Where Metz addressed the unconscious and its control of the cinematic experience, Mulvey was concerned with how 'the unconscious of patriarchal society has structured film form' (1992: 22). Her aim was to reveal classical or 'illusionistic' narrative cinema as being structured around visual pleasure and the sexual imbalance that determines it, in order to conceive of an oppositional film practice. Where Metz saw cinema as fetishistic, Mulvey emphasised the glaring gender issues at stake within his version of filmic reassurance: that it is the small boy who fears and the female who threatens. Mulvey built her argument through the staging of several points. Firstly, she established cinema as based on 'two contradictory aspects of the pleasurable structures of looking' (1992: 26): objectification (through scopophilia: the love of looking) and identification (through narcissism: the fascination with the self-image). But these two forms of visual pleasure, like the world, are 'split between active/male and passive/female' (1992: 27). The man looks or gazes, the woman is gazed at, indeed film ascribes her (and her alone) 'to-be-looked-at-ness' (ibid.). In this way, for Mulvey, the transcendental spectator is male. The image is organised around the visual pleasure he takes in the female form, which he enjoys often through the objectifying (and frequently fetishising) gaze of his on-screen surrogate, the male-lead. He objectifies the female characters presented to him, and identifies with the male characters (especially in their objectification of the female). Thus, even the illusion of agency attributed to the spectator is not available to the woman. All subjects are powerless but some are more powerless than others.

To recap, then, the film apparatus produces the subject and positions the spectator as false author of the image. The film unfolds as an illusion before the spectator who accepts its artificiality as real. The spectator occupies this position not just through the physical set up of the auditorium, or visual construction of the image, but because the cinematic experience recalls and replicates much earlier processes of subject formation, it enacts an 'artificial regression' (Baudry 1986: 313). This subject/spectator 'exists' in a hypothetical place created by the apparatus. At the same time, this subject/spectator is labelled as male, and the image constructed – as well as the psychic processes it invokes – is structured by sexual difference.

These conclusions/assumptions also lay beneath the second trajectory of 1970s film criticism, textual analysis, which associated theorists who favoured close-readings of individual films as a means to expose the spectator as ideological construct, as without agency. For them it was the film text that governed subjectivity, positioning the spectator as false author of the accepted illusion, and the film text that recalled and re-enacted formative psychological processes. But how did the film text do these two things? The discussion of the ideology of film textuality, as Melvyn Stokes and Richard Maltby point out (2001: 2), had two focuses. Like apparatus theory, textual analysis would take an increasing interest in psychoanalysis, but its initial moves were dictated by the semiotic theory of literature and, in particular, how the textual system – the text's various structures of signification – interacted with the reader. To understand this fully we must return to Saussurian semiotics and our still soggy hanky.

Sign = Signifier + Signified

A basic or linguistic sign is the sum of the word attributed to something and the meaning attributed to something. There is nothing about the emplacement of the letters s-o-g-g-y h-a-n-k-y (the signifier) that means wet paper tissue (what is signified). The relationship between signifier and signified is arbitrary and depends upon the application of (here, linguistic) conventions or codes *by the reader* to make meaning. Structuralism's task was to reveal these codes and consider the reader's activity in applying them. It was Roland Barthes, another French (non-film) theorist, who broadened this simple system of signification. For him, the sign's meaningfulness was not to be seen as a closed system ending with the signified. Rather, the signified was to be taken as a signifier in its own right. Barthes drew attention to the way that language, one system of signs, enters necessarily (during speech or public expression) into social practice, another system of signs, and thus the chain of signification journeys on. My initial use of the 'soggy tissue/sad friend' scenario is saturated with just this kind of meaning-liberation as 'wet paper tissue' becomes a signifier itself, loaded with emotional and interpersonal indications. The codes that determine our reading of signs power a chain of signification that allows us to read various levels of meaning: from primary signification's basic denotation of something (for example, wet paper tissue) to secondary/tertiary signification's more florid social connotations (for example, red-eyed, sore-nosed, miserable friend). While this might sound like the realm of an (all-too) active reader, this will prove to be far from the case.

In *S/Z*, which initially came out the same year as Althusser's article, Barthes focused upon the productivity of the reader in the making of meaning. He distinguished between the 'writerly' text, in which the reader is productive, and the classical 'readerly' text in which 'he' merely consumes. For Barthes, the goal of literary work is 'to make the reader no longer a consumer, but a producer of the text' (1974: 4). While the reader's role here in interpreting signs – a gesture of agency – is important, the key issue is the general productivity of textual signification. Barthes rejected the finite-ness of the signified and privileged the writerly text as 'a galaxy of signifiers' (1974: 5). Applying Barthes' ideas to film, textual analysts, through their attention to the many structures of signification (for example, narrative, genre, sound, editing, *mise-en-scène*), would reveal the 'galaxy of signifiers' inherent within the film text.

Let us take for example Clint Eastwood's character, Joe, in the opening scene of *A Fistful of Dollars*, looking down on the action unfolding before him. The narration tells us that he is a stranger riding into town. He has taken up his position by the well and watches the 'bandits' mistreating a child and a man, as a woman looks on concernedly from behind a barred window.

The genre iconography tells us that this is a western, that Clint Eastwood is the lone cowboy who rides into town and intervenes into an unjust situation, usually with a woman involved. In terms of sound, the non-diegetic music also tells us that this is a western, the lack of dialogue confirming the shifting of meaning to other registers. As Joe watches the action the music gains an implicit synchronicity, its simple but tension-filled phrasing mapping onto the increasing threat to the child and man, and Joe's (and our) growing curiosity. In terms of editing, the shot/reverse-shots establish dynamics between the parties, constructing the triangulation of Joe, the bandits and the woman. The two axes of action, one between the bandits and the well, the other between the woman and the well, intersect at Eastwood's character identifying him as what could be called the nexus of action, the most important figure. In terms of costumes, there is the clear distinction of the genre's goodies and baddies by their apparel – the hirsute bandits in dark rough hues, the woman (and child and man) in white cotton. The stubble-faced sandy-skinned lone cowboy operates, as expected, between the two: pulled between the shoot-outs and the love of a good woman. The stark contrast between good and bad, and the as

Fig. 1 *A Fistful of Dollars*: the stranger rides into town

yet uncommitted cowboy, is played out by the various movements from the right to the left of the frame. We look on, with the cowboy, through the high-angle shots from the well: his authority and threat contained for the time being behind its wooden frame. As the scene progresses and the man gets beaten and the bandit notices the cowboy, Joe moves out of this internal frame, uncommitted no more. The rest, of course, is history.

What this analysis of the scene illustrates is the dense network of signification provided by the various textual strategies. The correspondences between their different registers or languages reveal two things: that they all make the same points (genre or sound or costume, say, all support the general, and often more specific, plot details), and that there is a certain unboundedness of meaning, an endless array of meaning-making going on. However, what room for manoeuvre does the implied endlessness or elsewhere-ness of meaning leave for the spectator? Summoned into existence by an acknowledgement of the reader's place within the system of a text's meaningfulness (through Structuralism), the reader/spectator is emptied of agency as the endless number of meaning-making structures overwhelmed the significance of any one system or of any one player (the advent of post-Structuralism). Structuralism's assertion of the various codes affecting the reader becomes post-structuralism's 'innumerable possibilities of meaning' determining 'his' interpretation (Abrams 1981: 150). This 'infinite intercourse of codes' (Barthes 1981: 45) renders the reader *a site* through which the controlling systems of conventional thought shape the meaning 'he' generates. Post-structuralism undermined the subject's independence or agency, instead finding 'him' at the interface of numerous, endless, influencing factors, and false author of the image. As with apparatus theory, this post-structuralist textual analysis while seeming to attribute identity and agency to the film spectator, immediately voided him or her of actual presence or effect.

I have raced ahead somewhat in this post-structuralist discussion of writerly texts, which oppose the traditional, classical narratives yet sustain a still-passive reader. It is definitely worth returning to Barthes' identification of the classical readerly text as a more primary starting point in the semiotic discussion of the traditionally 'positioned' reader, the transcendent but powerless subject. The ideas of another linguist become crucial here. Emile Benveniste (1971) posed two important distinctions that underlay discussions about textual narration and ideology. Firstly, he distinguished between the enunciation, *l'énonciation*, and the enounced, *l'énoncé*. Enunciation, similar to 'articulation', points more to the subject speaking, who and where they are, where the enounced points more to what is articulated, as a meaningful set of words. The two could be thought of, then, as the difference between the context and the content of what is said. Secondly, Benveniste distinguishes between story (*histoire*) and discourse (*discours*), which is like the difference between third-person and first-person speech in terms of the subjectivity and authority implied. While Benveniste saw *discours* and *histoire* as separate, literary theorists working in a Marxist tradition (like Barthes and Julia Kristeva) saw them as absolutely involved, indeed at the heart of the impression of ideology. As Richard Allen puts it, they saw 'the novel as a form of *histoire* that conceals itself as *discours*' (1995: 41). In the 'classical' text the authorial voice (the enunciation) is concealed, and the reader steps in as transcendental subject. In this way, the transcendental reader became a product of the text itself.[6] This is just what Metz was saying, albeit via the film apparatus, in 'Story/Discourse': that in the concealment of the means of projection, the spectator is able to step in and 'own' the vision. The question that arises is how the film text, or rather the film narration – its storytelling – conceals its enunciation, and its role as discourse, in favour of creating the spectator as the site of the film's intelligibility.

A key way in which the classical film text was seen to conceal its enunciation or ideological status was through the distinction and discussion of the seamlessness of the classical text. Hollywood's developing practice of 'continuity' – its adherence to various rules of editing like the 180-degree rule, 30-degree rule, use of cuts, matches on action, shot/reverse-shot – worked to erase the palpability of the technical for the spectator, through both suppression and repetition of style as well as spectatorial habituation. (That we are suddenly looking down from what must be a crane shot does not interrupt our viewing because we are both distracted by the plot and accustomed to such things.) The classical Hollywood system thus promoted and perpetuated a narration style that could easily be taken as true, and a gaze that could be smoothly appropriated as our own. However, the conclusions emanating from apparatus theory and from film semiotics were not enough to explain the particularities of actual film texts, especially those that broke with seamlessness: their range of discontinuities (and their ideological management) and solicitation of character identifications beyond prescribed patterns. The image's formal features, such as framing, sequencing and the narrator's seeming 'invisibility' represented, according to Nick Browne, an ensemble of ways that authority implicitly positions the spectator/reader' (1986: 118). The eye of the camera roamed, the spectator was aligned with its masterful gaze but was also made to share characters' perspectives. But how could the spectator's omnipotence be guaranteed across this kind of mobility? How did the film text maintain the spectator's imaginary relation to the screen?

Drawn from Lacanian psychoanalysis (particularly Jacques-Alain Miller's interpretation), the notion of suture, and of the suturing of the subject into film discourse, seemed to offer the answer to these questions. Suture theory privileged secondary or character identification, where Metz subordinated it, as a way of reconciling the shifting gazes of the camera (sometimes omniscient, sometimes a character's point-of-view) (Miller 1977/78). Jean-Pierre Oudart, in the pages of *Cahiers du cinéma* in 1969, would apply the notion of suture to film, which would then be added to by Daniel Dayan (see Oudart 1990; Dayan 1976). A complex theory, suture is best understood through the two writers' example of the shot/reverse-shot. In the initial shot of the shot/reverse-shot sequence, the film offers the point of view of an 'ideal' off-screen character. The screen fills with an 'all-seeing' gaze that is not the spectator's and, as a result, the spectator is thrown out of 'his' position of transcendence. Suddenly aware of the frame, 'that his possession of space was only partial, illusory' (Dayan 1976: 448), the spectator is shaken from 'his' simple pleasure in the fecundity of 'his' own vision. The position of transcendence, of the 'Absent One', as Oudart called it, is owned elsewhere. However, in the next shot, the reverse-shot, the gaze is owned by an on-screen character and the spectator is restored to 'his' all-powerful place. As Daniel Dayan explained:

> The absent-one's glance is that of a nobody which becomes (with the reverse-shot) the glance of a somebody (a character present on screen). Being on-screen he can no longer compete with the spectator for the screen's possession. The spectator can resume his previous relationship with the film. The reverse-shot has 'sutured' the hole opened in the spectator's imaginary relationship with the filmic field by his perception of the absent-one. This effect and the system which produces it liberates the imaginary of the spectator, in order to manipulate it for its own ends. (1976: 449)

The suture represents the cut (or more aptly, the 'treated' cut): the film technique that stands in for the subject's lack of agency. It covers over 'his' loss of transcendence, represented by the off-screen character's superior vision. While Oudart and Dayan isolated the shot/reverse-shot structure (so prevalent in classical narrative film) as the site of suture, other theorists – in particular Stephen Heath – found it had a broader currency. In his article, 'Narrative Space', Heath located it against the lack posed (but covered) in the film's 'movements, its framings, its cuts, its intermittences' (1986: 403). In this sense, suture could be seen as pertaining to (the recovery of) all the moments when spectators become aware of the illusion, when they are reminded of their roles as passive, manipulated subjects, rather than all-powerful envision-ers. Film frequently stages, cannot help but stage, the spectator's loss in order to stage, too, 'his' regaining. Film techniques, like the shot/reverse-shot, re-gain the spectator's illusion of transcendence and of agency but cannot help but represent the loss at the same time. Accompanied by a scar, sutures – cuts, elipses – are precisely those things that 'mark' the narrative as 'seamless'. The suture, then, represents what is lacking and regained, absent and present, gone and here. Indeed, this is a fine pointer to its psychoanalytic heritage. As Kaja Silverman (1983), and later Richard Allen (1995), point out, the psychoanalytic notion of suture has much in common with the *fort/da* game, dwelt on by Freud, which provides another early/formative self-cohering scenario, which the film as text (rather than apparatus) recreates.

In this game the infant re-creates the departure and reappearance of 'his' mother – her absence as 'gone' (fort) and presence as 'there' (da) – through the throwing away and regaining of inanimate objects of which, as Freud asserts, 'there is no doubt that the greater pleasure was attached to the second act' (1991a: 284). Seen as the primary paradigm for mastery, but also, as Lacan stresses, for entrance into language, it is likened to the spectator's experience of this illusory disruption. The spectator's initial loss of transcendence is like the child's first *'fort'*, and the spectator's re-possession of this position, through the reverse-shot's location of the character's look, is like the child's utterance of *da*. As Richard Allen explains:

> In this way the lack upon which the subject's relationship to cinematic discourse is founded – the position of the Absent One – is elided. The spectator's anticipation of the second image and recollection of the first binds the spectator into the discourse of the film in a manner that parallels the suturing of the subject into language. (1995: 34–5)

As the discussion of spectatorship developed, suture – or a relative of it (and disavowal is certainly familial) – would figure in its various psychoanalytic debates, especially in terms of its function as psychological salve or treatment. In chapter four we shall be returning to this functionality, although far more cynically and far from psychoanalysis. For now, what I want to emphasise is that suture, which is all about guaranteeing the spectator's illusionistic relation to film, is a process of recovery, as the *fort/da* parallel makes clear. Suture locates recovery, as an illusion-based process of anxiety-ridden self-coherence, at the heart of spectatorship. Suture represents a merging of practical and textual influences, but other formative psychological processes were recalled and re-enacted within the (discourse of the classical) film text as well. Cinema, after all, often stages the dramas of growing up and rites of passage, as well as centralising them in their ideological intent. It comes as no surprise then that numerous, if not all, Hollywood narratives – from *Bringing Up Baby* (1938) to *The Graduate* (1967) – were found to revolve around the resolution of Oedipal dramas. In such narratives, the male protagonist would reject his immature ways, or a mother figure, and take up his rightful position in society, opposite a correct object of desire, and often to become a father himself. Overlain with gender trouble, such narrative processes will fall within our scrutiny of patriarchal discourse in the next chapter, where, again, the ideological text traces and confirms the correct, the comfortable, progression of the subject via the spectator's unwavering identification with its 'Oedipalised' heroes.

The two formative trajectories of spectatorship studies discussed here, one embracing the generalities of the apparatus, the other the seeming specificities of the text, should not be seen as discrete categories. Much of the work, and many of the major theorists, bridged the two. Metz's writing launched both the structural analysis of film and the psychoanalytic study of cinema. Mulvey's writings on visual pleasure combined an urgent reconsideration of the apparatus with a detailed scrutiny of the film text. In this first chapter I have wanted to capture the salient points about the transcendental spectator generated by these writers and have not been concerned, yet, with the local confusions or muddy logic of some of their denser moments. As the discussion develops below, however, much of this mud will resurface within it. I do want to delineate the overarching problems with these initial theories and how they have been challenged within the various critical spokes radiating out from them. Firstly, and perhaps the most obvious problem, is the assumption that all spectators are the same, the same over time, and male. Secondly, that all films, or at least all 'classical' films, are the same. Thirdly, that all spectators are powerless: they cannot resist the sways, the often sadistic sways, of the text. In lacking agency, they are *done to*: and being done to, so the theory goes, is a bad thing, to be avoided and denied.

Several routes of response to these problems would emerge to counter the classical model of spectatorship, especially its ahistoricism, its abstractness and its reification of the power of ideology. Spectators were found, at various points of film history, to be capable of resistance, of multiple readings and of counter or perverse interests. Whether emphasising the empirical, the historical or the ethnographic, spectators were revealed in their multifarious gender, class and ethnic affiliations. My concern in this book lies not with demonstrating the impossibility of asserting meaning for the ever-changeable spectator, but to persevere in comprehending the spectatorial experience via the triangulation of textual practices, psychic processes and social contexts. As such, for our purposes, what emerges from the previous discussion and its broad assumptions are three key issues that are to be taken up in the rest of the book, and that might, for the sake of concision, be called 'the three Ds'. The issue of *difference*: how the gender of the spectator, as one example, impacts upon spectatorship. The issue of *done-to-ness*: how the problem of submission for the spectator needs to be re-considered with regard to post-liberation culture (of women, of gays, of 'sex') and the pleasures of submission. The issue of *disavowel*: how spectatorship as self-affirming or salve requires a denial of, and distance from, various anxious implications that it, at the same time, depends upon.

2   SPECTATORSHIP AND DIFFERENCE: GENDER AND THE RUB OF SUBMISSION

The classical model of spectatorship that emerged in the 1970s set the terms for subsequent discussions of the subject, and, in fact, of film itself. Although intrinsically flawed in its generalisations, in speaking for all spectators without regard to personal, social or historical specificities, the central issue that it introduced – the relationship between cinema and ideology – would continue to characterise the debate on the spectatorial experience even as those conditions, or contexts, surrounding (or, rather, determining) spectatorship gained in prominence.

A major problem with the classical model and its assertion of a hypo-thetical all-inclusive spectator-subject, was its failure to address difference: how differences between spectators meant that there were different ways of experiencing film. So, for example, a San Francisco socialite's encounter with *Singin' in the Rain*, at its opening night in 1952, varies greatly from that of a Yorkshire Dales socialist worker watching daytime TV in 2002. Laura Mulvey in her 1975 *Screen* article made the crucial intervention of isolating the impact of sexual difference on spectatorship, but her ideas still traded on 'unitary' principles (Williams 1994: 3), they still generalised the spectator's response. For Mulvey the spectator-subject and, more importantly, 'his' gaze, was always male and thus continued the preemi-nence of a singular, unavoidable way of engaging with narrative cinema. What Mulvey did, however, was to firmly instate gender as a primary theme within the debate on spectatorship, thereby prioritising the discussion of difference within the evolution of film studies. In this chapter we will trace the evolving discussion of sexual difference and spectatorship, after

Mulvey, and consider how it reshaped the debate on individual agency in terms of gender. To begin with, let us return to Mulvey's thesis and its key but controversial conclusions.

Mulling over Mulvey

In confirming cinema as an ideological institution, Mulvey named that ideology as patriarchy and exposed the various ways in which classical narrative cinema endowed men with a litany of empowerment (subjectivity-activity-dominance) and entrapped women in the opposing qualities. This bias was achieved through both the mechanism of the gaze (via the apparatus) and the conceits of the narrative (via the text). As such, Mulvey's ideas bridged the two trajectories of 1970s film theory; indeed she intervened on each front of the emerging model of spectatorship and in so doing should be seen to have refashioned rather than rebuilt the system.

The resounding charge of 'Visual Pleasure and Narrative Cinema' was that the hypothetical spectator-subject was male. There was nothing incidental or inclusive about the 'he' inhabiting the work of Baudry, Metz and others: it was the accurate affirmation of the patriarchal pedigree of the institution of cinema (and, frequently, intellectualism) but an affirmation not yet made explicit. Mulvey, in making it explicit, asserted that the position of transcendence was available to the male spectator only, whose gaze was summoned and guided by the structural and sexual lures of the frame. It was his look that was solicited and his ego that was salved by the film's various formal and psychological strategies. These strategies revolved, primarily, around the female spectacle. She functioned as both the locus for harnessing that male gaze and as the trigger for the re-enactment of his formative psychic processes.

According to Mulvey, classical narrative cinema works through the elicitation of two forms of visual pleasure, two forms that compose and deter-mine the gaze as male: objectification and identification. The gaze objectifies female characters and identifies with male characters; it desires the female and aspires to the male. The centrality and allure of the female form in film is established through characterisation (the exposition of the heroine as 'hot property') and camera work (movement, framing and so on, which create her as the focus of 'erotic contemplation' (1992: 27)). So, content and form work together to create and satisfy the sexually-laden viewing pleasures of the male – that is the heterosexual male – spectator. At the same time, this spectator is aligned with the male protagonist, again through, say, characterisation (his propelling of narrative action) and camera work (which favours his subjective experience in, for example, restricted narration or point-of-view shots). Classical narrative cinema privileges the male protagonist's actions, interests (not least, in women) and existential experience, channelling its thematic preoccupations, and the spectator's will to identify, through his character.

By way of example, let us take a close look at Grace Kelly's entrance in *Rear Window* (1954), in which her utter beauty is both staggeringly self-evident and cinematically entrenched. On a balmy New York evening, a chair-ridden, limb-plastered Jeffries (James Stewart) slumbers by his open window, chock-full of fantasies about his neighbours' lives. A medium shot shows his eyes drifting open in the half-light of a trance-like evening and the shadow of someone's approach rising up his face. In the following point-of-view shot, Lisa (Kelly) leans in to kiss him, the frame filling with this icon of female beauty. Such spectatorial bounty seems unsustainable – 'we' can share Jeffries' eyes but not his lips – and the cut to the side-on shot of the two kissing can only feel abrupt. However, Hitchcock does not simply maintain the pleasures of this scene but increases them. Filmed in the slightest slow motion, a just perceptible expansion of time, the kiss is weighted with the momentousness of lived experience, even as its aestheticisation increases.

The grainy haziness of the image, provided by filming the scene in close-up and double printing each frame in slow motion in order to prolong the kiss, gave 'the brief sequence a dreamy sensuality'.[1] These techniques, by Hitchcock and Robert Burks, his cinematographer, constructed the fantasy of the perfect kiss, securing Lisa's status as apparition and Jeffries' as (wet)dreamer. While the spectator is firmly aligned with Jeffries' experience, he is not limited by it: the male gaze is generated and anchored by the protagonist but also exceeds him.

Lisa literally freezes up the action in this scene, and, in the one that follows, continues an almost clichéd enactment of Mulvey's formulations of the female as spectacle. After Jeffries' and Lisa's romantic, if eccentric, conversation which ends in Jeffries' question 'who are you?' Lisa introduces herself through a succession of self-spotlighting. She moves from one lamp in the room to another, giving part of her name as each is switched on.

Fig. 2 *Rear Window*: the fantasy of the perfect kiss

Finally, revelation complete, she poses, model-like, centre-frame. Her full identity has rested upon our ability to see her, is inextricably bound to her role as image and as exhibitionist. She does not just 'connote *to-be-looked-at-ness*' (Mulvey 1992: 27), she lives it. At the same time, Jeffries' status as surrogate for the spectator could not be more pronounced: seated in a darkened room, immobilised with his visual function privileged, he can but succumb to the spectacle. His incapacity, his impotence – and he himself declares his love-life inactive – raises interesting questions about male virility (to be considered later), but, more importantly, further marks the scene as sexual fantasy. After all, heterosexual pornography often depends upon rendering the out-of-your-league woman available to the more limited man. The scene's erotic economy is also funded by its supporting formal strategies, which enact the construction of (male) arousal/erection. The ascending scales sung in the background as Jeffries falls asleep, and the mounting shadow of Lisa's approach, represent a 'build-up' that is some-what satisfied in the climactic kiss. That this is followed by Lisa's introduction from 'top-to-bottom', from head to toe, the ascent and descent are marked complete. On a range of levels, then, the scene conveys the gaze as male, as desire-laden and as heterosexual.

Classical narrative cinema constructs 'woman as image, man as bearer of the look' (ibid.). The man has a mission, the woman is tempting distraction. He drives the narrative, she stills it. He has depth, she is surface. This fundamental disparity along the plane of gender and agency consolidates classical cinema's re-creation of the 'sexual imbalance' of wider society. In other words, cinema merely replicates broader inequities. More importantly, however, this fundamental disparity, like the 'repressive apparatus' of Marxist analysis, is a self-perpetuating or self-regulating system. An ideological homeostasis, it operates through, and depends upon, the psychological processes of subject formation and fortification played out in, and through, film. In underlying the two forms of visual pleasure, these processes – the mirror stage and fetishism – must, according to Mulvey, now be read as patriarchal.

While for Freud and Lacan the mirror phase was unmarked by sexual differentiation (which occurred later, developmentally), Mulvey, in confirming its centrality to the spectatorial experience, marks it as male.[2] Cinema is a site of interpellation but it is the male subject that it calls forth. It is the male protagonist who is offered up for the (male) spectator's (mis)-recognition, who provides that more competent, more in-control image of the spectator's like. It is the male star who, for Mulvey, represents that 'more perfect, more complete, more powerful ego ideal conceived in the original moment of recognition in front of the mirror' (1992: 28). Classical narrative cinema solicits and privileges a male experience, idealising the male protagonist and the male gaze that incorporates him. Jeffries, as my analysis above illustrated, provides a clear example. Cinema, then, provides our most common mirror, reviving the conditions of, and 'older fascination' with, looking that was deemed so inseparable from our developing subjectivity. But, and this is crucial, it is the male subject that is summoned and nurtured through it. Through both apparatus and text the male protagonist is set up as the primary source of identification, through mechanics (via perspective), content (via the male existential experience) and psychology (via narcissistic identification).

Fetishism as male practice

Beyond the obvious wish-fulfilling functions of Jeffries' (wet) dream, the role of woman as image needs to be seen as bound up with reassuring the male spectator about the threat that woman represented. For Mulvey, woman exists only 'in relation to castration' (1992: 22); she cannot help but embody the possibility of male disempowerment. Thus her cinematic construction, whether in terms of spectacle or narrative, always stems from a 'making safe' agenda. Both the coding of her appearance and the progression of her character are rooted in rendering the female unthreatening. Mulvey would delineate two routes emanating from this agenda, two escape routes out of this frightful situation, but before exploring these, let us recall briefly the psychoanalytic concept upon which castration anxiety is based.

In Freud's theory of Fetishism, the small boy fears that he, like his mother, will lose his penis, or have it taken away, so he tries to cover over her loss by over-valuing some other part of her body or some other related object by creating a fetish (Freud 1991d). Indeed, Freud suggested that this relatedness might spring, simply, from the fear-ridden child's averted gaze: hence the relative prevalence of foot or shoe fetishism. Where, for Metz, this compensatory mechanism represented cinema's covering over of the absence of reality with the heightened illusion, for Mulvey, the primacy of sexual difference to the fetishistic reflex could not be overlooked or overstated. The cover-up job was, instead, distinctly patriarchal. Spectatorship still represented a desire-fuelled but anxiety-ridden relation to the screen but the lack that was being worked out, or played out, by cinema was the female's lack and the fretful reality that it represented to the male. At stake in the belief/disbelief, there/not there economy of illusion-based narrative film (though Metz spoke of all film) was male anxiety, and male anxiety rooted in and acted out upon the female body. According to Mulvey there were two ways that this anxiety was conveyed and countered within narrative film and its female body or bodies. On one hand, through objectification or voyeurism, the woman was, literally, put in her place. She was undone by way of removing her mystery, by possessing and/or punishing her. On the other hand, her threat or potency was undermined or broken up by way of fragmenting and fetishising her body.

She is undone I: possession and punishment

Objectification fuels the 'gotta-get-the-girl' principle underwriting classical cinema's visual and narrative properties, and the related motivations of male characters and spectators. This principle can be thought of as a capturing of the woman on several levels – as aesthetic image by the camera, as prized partner by the male protagonist or as guilty party by the comeuppance/socially moral narrative. This progression from the first, most local, of these levels to the last one's collective harnessing of the female can be thought of as inscribing a move from spectacle to narrative, and from the particular to the general. It is a move that, in representing the expansion from the individual woman to all women, encapsulates the sexist or patriarchal project rather than the status of such women as 'special cases'. Classical Hollywood endlessly recounted this kind of emplacement or fixing of women, a subjection or subjugation that Mulvey saw as sadistic. We will be returning to this issue and its mobilisation of a key element of spectatorial agency – the relationship between sadism and masochism – in the next chapter. However, for now, let us light this first escape route, as Mulvey did, through a discussion of film noir. This 'genre' provides the perfect example in its intensification of the patriarchal plot through combining the possession principle of the romance trajectory with the investigation-castigation principle of the crime narrative.[3]

In both the classic *noirs* of the 1940s and 1950s and the contemporary erotic thriller, the doomed femininity of the female protagonist, the femme fatale, is inscribed through the dual themes of criminal investigation and physical desire. In countless examples ethereal beauties are revealed as ambitious gold-diggers, their smoky sensualities increasingly exposed as the mercenary tactics of a calculating mind. In *The Killers* (1946), for example, the misdeeds of the ever-absent but oft-conjured Kitty (Ava Gardner) are steadily suggested until their final dramatic disclosure in which she pleads with her dying-then-dead husband to clear her name before he goes. Starting with the murder of Swede (Burt Lancaster) the narrative then traces an insurance investigator's search for Swede's killers through the interweaving of interviews and extended flashbacks. Having met the assassins in the film's first sequences, it is clear that the titular killers are elsewhere. The steady piecing together of information reveals how a web of highly suspect characters and dodgy acts encircles Swede's death, but that one person is the most guilty: the femme fatale who had hooked and betrayed him. The final emphasis rests upon Kitty's overwhelming crime in contrast to the explicit criminality of the other thieves and rogues. In this sense the 'killers' of the title is Kitty, or rather, are all women. A similar investigatory narrative, and 'patriarchal unconscious', underlies most *noirs* and neo-*noirs*. Films like *Double Indemnity* (1944), *Out of the Past* (1947) and *D.O.A.* (1950), *Body Heat* (1981) or *Body of Evidence* (1992) function not so much as 'whodunnits' but as 'shedunnits', which readily become 'theydunnits', in which the 'they' is women in general.

Body of Evidence provides an excellent contemporary example in its ex-cessive rendering of the *noir* world and its gender lessons.[4] In it, Madonna plays Rebecca Carlson who is charged with her boyfriend's death. Willem Defoe plays her lawyer, Frank Delaney, who falls for, defends, and is – of course – deceived by her. The implicitly sexualised threat of the femme fatale becomes Rebecca's explicit penchant for sadomasochism (accentuated by Madonna's *Sex*iness).[5] In addition, with the prosecution's suggest-ion that the victim died during, and because of, his sexual encounter with Rebecca, her body during her trial is called the 'murder weapon itself'. Rebecca is only 'known' and undone in the final scene, where her death works to both mark and merge her demystification and punishment in still strikingly sexualised terms. To 'know' the femme fatale and to punish her entwine as part of the same logic. Frank enters her home after the trial to find Rebecca taunting and rejecting Dr Paley (Jürgen Prochnow), a key witness for the defence and, it is now revealed, another lover. While dismissing Frank too, Paley shoots Rebecca in what can be seen, especially in the film's pornographic predisposition, as the movie's cum-shot.

Indulging the soft-core of popular cinema, and as a showcase for Madonna, *Body of Evidence* provides many sex scenes which focus on Rebecca and Frank's sexual adventure. Frank is, unusually for cinematic sex but appropriately for *noir*, the one done to. Rebecca, 'on top' here, as in all aspects of their relationship, calls the shots, drips the wax, wins the case. Frank takes it, gratefully. The close-ups on his face and expressions – bewilderment, impatience, wonder – are the conventional codes for conveying feminised pleasure (Patton 1989: 105). But when Paley fires at Rebecca, her spectacular death – in which she is blasted through her French window to land in the water below – re-instates male phallic authority. The return to order, the firing, returns and reprioritises masculine sexual pleasure. It is the climax of the film, the cum-shot, for 'male sexual fulfilment, in Western culture, is synonymous with orgasm ... No orgasm, no sexual pleasure. No cum-shot, no narrative closure' (Patton 1989: 104).

The femme fatale's threat has been contained, not only in the personal terms of the diegesis but through the general terms of sexual politics and its filmic hinterland. The conclusion of *Body of Evidence* reinstates both the normative family (Delaney's wife is shown awaiting him) and justice (the guilty party dies). But it also depicts the desire for the cum-shot – the death of Rebecca – as a communal experience with the camera positioned directly facing her. According to Cindy Patton, talking about pornography, 'the cinematic conventions which position the viewer as the person coming are fairly seamless ... regardless of your anatomical configuration' (ibid.). Just as it is 'easy to imagine that this is your penis' (ibid.), it is also easy to imagine that this is your gun. In this way, the spectator is, in terms of authority, sexual potency and complicity, phallically aligned with the ultimate possession and punishment of the femme fatale.

She is undone II: bits and pieces

An alternative though often contiguous means for diminishing the female threat on film was provided by the breaking up of her body from a complete to a partial whole, and through an overvaluation of these 'parts' or of other things that stood in for them. The woman's body was fragmented or fetishised in this way and in so doing castration was disavowed 'by the substitution of a fetish object or turning the represented figure into a fetish so that it becomes reassuring rather than dangerous (hence overvaluation, the cult of the female star)' (Mulvey 1992: 29). An alternative kind of possession, this 'fetishistic scopophilia' glorified or valued the physical beauty of the object to make it satisfying in itself: the mere act of looking removed from any anxious implications. The fetishistic representation of the woman is obvious in many classical narrative films and has been associated with certain female stars, or with the work of certain directors. For example, critics have noted the overvaluation of, or the particular visual obsession with, parts of certain women's bodies: Garbo's lips, Hepburn's cheekbones, Marilyn's breathy voice have been distinguished as iconic qualities of these stars but also as testimony to the common-compensatory fragmentation of their bodies. Alternatively, threatening (that is, castrating) women are associated with phallic objects which stand in for that which is missing at the same time as referencing phallic authority that is only ever on loan. A striking example is provided by Rita Hayworth in *Gilda* (1946).

Fig. 3 *Gilda*: Rita Hayworth,
the fiery femme fatale

Her body taut within the sheath-like dress, the cigarette holder extended erect away from her, sleek and two-tone, Hayworth almost resembles a cigarette holder herself: cigarette and receptacle both. This is not the gag of the popped cork or erupting champagne bottle that accompanies the cruder construction of Monroe, as in *Gentlemen Prefer Blondes* (1953), but the omnipresent phallic graphic. The fetishised object and its referencing of fear and threat become a shorthand sign for female murderousness elsewhere in cinema. Where guns have been 'allied with the intimate fabric of fetishism in the erotic thriller' (Williams 2005: 18) as well as their predecessors, this can also be seen to be epitomised by the ice-pick in *Basic Instinct* (1992). But the shorthand sign works equally well in the recent blockbuster *Chicago* (2002) to emphasise the thrilling threats posed by its central characters. While the female killers are celebrated, ultimately, this Broadway musical adaptation provides an excellent example of the fetishisation of the female and its enchanting blend of danger and desire. Its sexual self-consciousness arises not only from the sexual liberalisms of contemporary cinema but from those associated with the stage version's original choreographer Bob Fosse's work (Mizejewski 1992: 210).

The opening sequence of *Chicago* is an almost textbook case of the fetishisation of the female, or rather, it is exploited for a tantalisingly threatening effect. Velma Kelly (Catherine Zeta Jones) initiates the narrative, her stilettoed feet leaving a car. The frame then shows her shapely, stockinged legs approaching a nightclub door. The fragmentation of her body continues as she gets ready for her musical act: a medium close-up on her washing blood off her hands, alluding to the wound of castration, and her pulling on her tights in a scene that cannot help but reference Gilda's similar preparations to firmly construct the female spectacle. The spectator does not see Velma in her entirety until she is centre stage, in front of the – most noticeably – male audience. Also, it is only in the context of something missing (and a violent lack at that) that Velma is exposed: the emcee announces the fabulous Kelly Sisters, the lights hit the stage but Veronica, who Velma has just murdered, is absent.

The reason for Mulvey's impact and enduring status was quite simple: her claims made – and still do make – a lot of sense, for inequities between the sexes, between the exposition, stylisation and narrative status of male and female characters, are easily identifiable within classical Hollywood. However, cinema as a creative form and individuals as fickle things mean that the spectatorial experience can be a good deal more complicated than Mulvey allowed for: her conclusions were inadequate to account for all spectators, or indeed, for all films. At the heart of her thesis about classical cinema in 'Visual Pleasure and Narrative Cinema' were three controversial conclusions. One, women cannot be subjects; they cannot own the gaze (read: there is no such thing as a female spectator). Two, men cannot be objects; they cannot be gazed at, they can only look, and only at women (read: there is no such thing as a male spectacle). Three, the only way to evade conclusions one and two, for spectatorship to be liberated from patriarchal ideology, was via a film practice that operated in opposition to narrative cinema. Indeed, this would need to be a film practice that was not, in fact, narrative-based, for, as French feminists would elucidate, narrative itself was a tool of patriarchy (read: there is no such thing as non-patriarchal narrative cinema).[6] These three conclusions were taken to task by other theorists, and can be seen as the ancestry for the various 'anti-classical' trajectories of spectatorship studies. While the discussion of the more radical potential of narrative cinema provides a growing concern through chapters three and four, the gendering of spectatorial agency will continue as the structuring principle for the rest of this chapter.

After Mulvey – the Female spectator: how women look

In 'Visual Pleasure and Narrative Cinema' the women in the audience disappeared behind the predominating male storyline, characters and gaze as well as the urgency of classifying film as patriarchal. But what of those films that told of the female experience, passage or plight? How could Mulvey's thesis account for classical narratives clearly affording or directed towards women-centred pleasures? Unsurprisingly, the woman's film became an obvious focus for feminist film theorists: here, after all, was a 'genre' dependent upon and catering to a female audience. Even if, as Mary Ann Doane pointed out, there is something a tad suspect about the cordoning off of the 'woman's picture', 'as though the historical threat of a potential feminisation of the spectatorial position required an elaborate work of generic containment' (1987: 2). The trouble with the woman's film, however, was that while the screen and audience were populated by women, its heroines were either mired in misery or soon would be, the narratives having them teased by a happiness that would rarely stay theirs.

A key revision to Mulvey's argument came from Mulvey herself. In her 1981 follow-up piece, 'Afterthoughts on "Visual Pleasure and Narrative Cinema" inspired by *Duel in the Sun*', Mulvey both acknowledged the existence of the female spectator and attributed to her a degree of agency (1989: 29–38). But the situation was barely less bleak. Two options became available to the female spectator who would oscillate between them. She could identify with the inevitably passive and masochistic female character (as elucidated via the women's film) or she could, briefly, for the duration of a film only, borrow the male gaze and identify with the male character. In doing so she engaged in a kind of transvestism, she 'cross-gazed': the gaze remained male even though she wore it too. Mulvey's female spectator was, thus, characterised by discomfort and restlessness as she alternated between one defeating alignment and another, between identification with the masochistic 'heroine' and the ill-fitting garb of the male gaze.

Many other theorists became involved in debating the fixity of this female spectator's experience by describing the different positions that the female spectator could occupy or move between. These descriptions inevitably required a reconciliation of her (potential) subject-status, as pleasure-taking member of the audience, and object-status, as spectacle on-screen; of her capacity to identify with the 'to-be-defeated' female character, with whom she was 'naturally' aligned, and the male character, with whom her look would, necessarily, merge. The female spectator's relationship to these positions was variously defined and evaluated. As well as providing a range of characteristics and frames of reference for female spectatorship, these theorists helped initiate the important negotiation of the agency of women as consumers of popular culture or as creators of oppositional art.

The recurring sets of ideas within these still psychoanalytically-oriented discussions centred on female over-identification on the one hand, and spectatorial movement on the other: on exploring the alignments or affiliations between women, and the rigidity, or otherwise, of identification. Let us look at these more closely in order to trace a path through the various issues and key voices within the evolving debate on female spectatorship.

Where Mulvey's male spectator got to identify with the often noble but otherwise fortifying progression of the male protagonist, the female protagonist of the classical narrative offered the female spectator a far from recuperative path. Rather, as Doane put it, female identification in this model 'reinforc[ed] her submission' (1987: 16). This negative iteration was articulated through, and compounded by, the proximity of the female spectator to the image. Where the male spectator kept a therapeutic distance from the disempowerment that the female spectacle represented, the female spectator, in many ways, *was* the female spectacle, and hence unable to employ defensive mechanisms against her disempowerment, like disavowal. Excluded from fetishism in lacking the penis herself, she could but identify with the castrated woman. Without the 'biological foundation to engage in the sophisticated game of juggling presence and absence in cinematic representation' she was, according to Linda Williams, forced to over-identify, a relation to the image characterised by an excessive and none-too-healthy closeness (1990: 156).

This inherently female inability to 'take a distance' explained, for some, the propensity for women to cry at films – and a whole host of other over-emotion oriented flaws – and the very labelling of the woman's film as 'weepie'.[7] Primarily, however, the concept of female over-identification evidenced further the restraining fictions traded by patriarchal narrative film. Taken up by feminist theorists, over-identification became a tool for exposing and extending both this coercive rubric of classical Hollywood and the possible channels of escape.

Doane, Williams and Tania Modleski, for example, looked at how this dynamic between female spectator and female image is articulated *on*-screen, how films represent over-identification or an over-determined closeness between female characters, but did so with varying degrees of pessimism and/or commitment to the traditions of psychoanlaysis.

Doane, in 'Film and Masquerade', first published in 1982, found classical cinema to both open up and close down a space for the female spectator in 'narrativising the negation of the female gaze' (1999: 141). Films like *Dark Victory* (1939), *Now Voyager* (1942), *Leave Her to Heaven* (1945), *Humoresque* (1946) and *Beyond the Forest* (1949) with their staring, glaring, or bespectacled women, inscribed female subjectivity through the heroines' heightened looks, but always only temporarily. Like Mulvey, Doane saw no real way out for the classical female spectator, from the bind of either masochistic entrapment or a temporary, masculinity-on-loan. However, her distinction of femininity as masquerade, via Joan Riviere's article of 1929, suggested a more hopeful future in acknowledging the potential for women to resist or defy the patriarchal imperative. The masquerade, the recognition of the skilled performance of the excesses of femininity, represented the female spectator's ability to distance herself from the image. In so doing, the masquerade could 'generate a problematic within which the image is manipulable, producible and readable by the woman' (Doane 1999: 143). Like Mulvey again, Doane saw this problematic as only attainable within avant-garde cinematic practices; only a non- or anti-narrative cinema could intervene into the entrapment of over-identi-fication, to both generate and exploit this problematic in order to activate the agency of the female spectator. The critique of classical cinema was essential to this project, however, for it not only fuelled but determined the path of this oppositional practice: 'The tropes of female spectatorship are not empowering. But we need to understand the tropes of their physical appeal more fully before we can produce an effective alternative cinema' (1987: 9).

Modleski was interested similarly in filling out our understanding of these tropes through thinking about how women 'looked' and looked specifically at other women in film, but like an increasing number of theorists, she was not giving up on popular film entirely. Having identified a recurrent thematisation of female over-identification in Alfred Hitchcock's work, Modleski found this recurrence less a problem for women than for men and for Hitchcock in particular (1988: 1–15). Her aim in her 1982 essay on *Rebecca* (1940) was to expand the psychoanalytic repertoire of patriarchal descriptions of spectatorship by mapping the female Oedipal trajectory. Challenging Raymond Bellour's (1979) claim that all Hollywood narratives traced the male Oedipal story, Modleski reads *Rebecca* instead as a female Oedipal narrative based upon over-identification. In so doing, over-identification comes to describe not only the female spectator's relationship to the text, but the female character's destiny. A feminist intervention by Modleski, it is, however, crucial to note that this (classical) female Oedipal trajectory was operating also in the service of the patriarchal status quo. Let us return to Freud, as Modleski does, to make this female destiny clear.

Modleski's psychoanalytic reading of *Rebecca* – the story of a young woman's (the new Mrs De Winter's) appropriation of an older dead woman's (Rebecca's) life – reclaims the female Oedipal trajectory as the pattern and rubric for the development of its female heroine. Such a reading is based upon Freud's articulation, in his lecture on femininity, of the girl's passage to maturity. This passage, as the girl's 'change to femininity', is marked by her shift from the clitoris to the vagina as the site of sexual pleasure: a shift from a female-identified self-pleasure to a pleasure in penetration (1991c: 151). It is also marked by the transfer of her original attachment to her mother to her father: the male – the correct – object of desire. That this original attachment 'ends in hate' is essential to the transfer, for, as Freud asserts, the girl blames her mother for her own castrated state which she seeks to amend by gaining the father's penis or its substitute, a baby (1991c: 155).

Now, in narrative terms, woman's maturation, her eventual 'giving pref-erence to passive aims', is marked by allowing her to take up her rightful position as object of the male gaze (1991c: 149). In *Rebecca*, the maturation of the new Mrs De Winter – and so defined is she by her relationship to her husband and his first wife that she is never given her own name – follows her initial over-identification with, but eventual rejection of, the old Mrs De Winter. This female-narrative passage – her 'attempt to detach herself from the mother in order to attach herself to a *man*' – is what eventually allows the heroine to achieve happiness with her husband (Modleski 1988: 50). Rebecca's status as 'mother' is implicit in the infantilisation of her successor, the women's differences in age and authority and Mr De Winter's role as father figure to his new young wife. The rejection of Rebecca, of the new Mrs De Winter's obsessive and emulating (over)identification with her, is dramatically marked at closure as the spectre of the absent woman – represented by her rooms, her monogrammed possessions and devoted servant – is fully destroyed, consumed in fact by flames. The eradication of the old Mrs De Winter's name allows it to be owned by the new wife. As Mr and Mrs De Winter come together at the end of the film in front of the blazing house, the heroine is firmly and finally located next to her husband. She is held by his look, which is no longer distracted; by his arms, which are no longer busy with other things; by his affection, which is no longer ambiguous. For Doane, this ending repeats the denial of female subjec-tivity by eradicating finally the powerful Rebecca: powerful in her ability to cast her look and influence even beyond the grave, so that 'this denial of the absent woman and the resultant recuperation of presence form the basis for the reunification and harmony of the couple which closes the film' (1988: 210). For Modleski, it ends the process of socialisation for the young Mrs De Winter, moving her from her woman-centred identification with her predecessor to place her irrefutably with her husband. Modleski confirms the hegemonic restoration of closure, but also its potential ambi-guity, its grains of resistance, and the unruly force that the character of Rebecca represented: 'if death by drowning did not extinguish the woman's desire, can we be certain that death by fire has reduced it utterly to ashes?' (1988: 55).

In a different vein, Williams was intent on challenging the model of female spectatorship as either implicitly or ultimately negative. For her, the resounding charge of Doane's sentiments on the female spectator was that 'either way ... she loses herself' (1990: 154). For Williams, the conservatism of closure in the classical film (emphasised by Modleski) could easily be resisted by the female spectator. Williams, instead, located female pleasure within spectatorship and in the female spectator's capacity to occupy all the existing positions of identification (male as well as female, from the periphery as well as the protagonist). Through her reading of the maternal melodrama *Stella Dallas* (1937), she suggests how female characters and thus female spectators can engage in the sophisticated games arising from *their* voyeuristic distance from the image, a distance afforded not by anatomical difference (via fetishism), nor by masquerade (via avant-garde practice) but as a result of the knowingness and 'competence' arising from female socialisation and, specifically, mothering under patriarchy (1990: 155). Such games defy the female spectator's fixed, uninformed or purely submissive position, and resist the patriarchal imperative of the classical film.

> This manufacturing of distance, this female voyeurism-with-a-differ-ence, is an aspect of *every* female spectator's gaze at the image of her like. For rather than adopting either the distance and mastery of the masculine voyeur or the over-identification of Doane's woman who loses herself in the image, the female spectator is in a constant state of juggling all positions at once. (ibid.)

A typical multi-tasker, Williams' woman, her female spectator of narrative film, can inhabit the range of identificatory positions in an act that is both active and pleasurable but also inherently female and socially grounded. *Stella Dallas* might end with a familiarly tragic scenario for its heroine-victim – Joan Crawford's character in the cold harsh air of martyrdom catching a last look at her daughter – but, crucially, the female spectator does not 'acquiesce' to its prescription (ibid.). Williams moves beyond the psychoanalytic model to implicate women's complex but enabling sociali-sation outside the cinema: the spectator's social context.

The mobility of the spectator in identifying with different characters on-screen had proven integral to developing psychoanalytic theories of spectatorship, especially in terms of the gendering of the emerging lines of identification. Janet Bergstrom's earlier translation and application of Raymond Bellour's psychoanalytic discussions privileged his distinction of 'multiple identificatory positions', albeit that they still served the dominant discourse (1990: 181). This meant that the female spectator, like the male spectator, could inhabit various positions, or alignments with characters. The propensity for this non-gender-specific spectator to identify with multiple positions and Freud's essay, 'A Child is Being Beaten' from 1919, upon which this propensity was based, proved extremely fruitful for later critical work on spectatorial liberty, and we can see its impact within feminist-informed work such as Carol Clover on horror (1992), Linda Williams on sex films (1989) or Patricia White on 'retrospectatorship' (1999). However, this spectatorial mobility also had the potential to suggest a troubling levelling of the spectator's experience when things were clearly more complicated for girls. Indeed, the arguments being traced here are very much about recognising and negotiating the complexity of the female experience that was ignored in the initial masculinisation of her position, or underrated in this liberal freeing of the spectator. The more embroiled or unavoidable this negotiation was for psychoanalytic theory, the more stultifying psychoanalysis would become as feminists' theoretical tool of choice. That said, Elizabeth Cowie's (1979/80) (Lacanian) psychoanalytic reading of *Coma* (1978) provided a significant contribution in sustaining the female spectator's complexity. In it she argued that the heroine as both active investigator and potential victim allowed the female spectator to move between identifying with her controlling look and objectifying her in her inevitable submission. Identification, then, was not fixed by identity (by gender, for example) so much as it was determined by the structuring of looks within film, its narrative's 'narratingness' that engages and places the spectator. But while (gender) identity did not determine identification, it did inform it, along with the film's typically sexist sub-text. As such, the seemingly 'progressive' text, with its unusually feisty female, needed to be seen as masking – perhaps even licensing – the enduring, familiar, patriarchal plot.

Where the female spectator was acknowledged as alternating between different identificatory positions, Teresa de Lauretis argued in 1984 that identification involved movement itself.[8] For her, the female spectator, rather than moving between two different positions, occupies them both at the same time. De Lauretis's female spectator is involved in a 'double identification' (1999: 90): a figural narrative identification with both the mythical subject (of the apparatus) and narrative image (of the text).

Unlike the first set of (self-abnegating) identifications arising from the active/passive dichotomy of sexual difference, these figural identifications happen simultaneously: there can be no alternating between the one and the other for they are instead 'concurrently borne and mutually implicated by the process of narrativity' (ibid.). Unlike the first set too, they function outside of gender delineations. In this sense, double identification is inherently bisexual and by this de Lauretis meant that it involved both masculine and feminine perspectives. Or, at least, spectatorship had this capacity to be bisexual: for the first set, so caught up in the social world and the masculine versus feminine binary determining it, meant that identification was always framed by gender difference.

What emerges, repeatedly, are the theoretical hurdles surrounding the female spectator: the self-fulfilling problem of identifying her as a problem. Doane, speaking within the psychoanalytic tradition with which she was engaged, asks: 'why should it be the case that processes of identification and spectatorial engagement are more complicated (if not convoluted) for the female spectator than for the male? And why does it seem essential that a masculine position appear somewhere in the delineation of female spectatorship (in Mulvey's, de Lauretis's, and, for that matter, my own formulations)?' (1987: 6–7). Doane, thus, finds herself guilty of perpetuating this problematising of the female condition – even as she recognises 'problematising' for the fruitful act that it is.

So we begin to get a sense of the limitations of psychoanalytic theory, a certain theoretical circularity. Let us return to Williams' woman, her female spectator who comes over not as cross-eyed and oscillating, but in a productive state of flux. Her inherent fluidity results from her internal relation to the film's narrative, characters and image but, more importantly, from her external existence in the social sphere, which is characterised by the pull of competing or contradictory forces. Indeed, as Williams put it, 'the female spectator tends to identify with contradiction itself – with contradictions located at the heart of the socially-constructed roles of daughter, wife, *and* mother – rather than with the single person of the mother' (1990: 152). Williams was not the first to raise (or rather remind us of) the spectator's conditions of existence (indeed, the grand appropriation of Althusserian Marxism for psychoanalytic ends was a growing sore for theorists more engaged in the social critique of everyday life). The significance of the 'social' and its intrinsic complexities had been there from the start: Claire Johnston and Pam Cook's article on Raoul Walsh's films, first published in 1974, identified contradictions and distanciations in the figuring of the female even as it laid bare the psychic workings of the patriarchal text. Johnston's pamphlet on women's cinema, a year earlier, decried Hollywood's production of such texts, but acknowledged its value as entertainment and, as 'a two-way process', its lessons for feminist filmmakers (1991: 31). In terms of spectatorial agency, the ever canny B. Ruby Rich would write in 1978 that 'texts [can] be transformed at the level of reception and not ... fall into a trap of condescension toward our own developed powers as active producers of meaning' (1990: 278). In casting the textual spectator against the real woman in the audience, Williams also drew upon Rich who likened woman's experience to that of an exile, eternally embroiled in a dialectic of cultural opposition: forever both inside and outside of culture (ibid.). To reconcile, explain or embrace the contradictions inherent in female spectatorship, in the female experience, in gender representation – of activity and passivity, entrapment and mobility, inside and outside, subjectivity and victimhood – required a move on from the sexual subject of psychoanalysis towards the social subject.

The social subject

As the female spectator emerged as a contradictory figure grounded in the complexities of her social formation which were articulated on-screen and lived off-screen, the psychoanalytic model of spectatorship ceased to be an adequate or accurate means of understanding her. Increasing emphasis was placed, instead, on more material conditions and how individuals' cultural context or diverse identities impacted upon spectatorship: how their agency in reading was determined by things beyond the regimes of the text. While the potential for female spectators to 'read against the grain' – to not succumb to/naturally resist texts' patriarchal prescriptions – had seasoned the work of Cook, Johnston, Williams and Rich with an optimism absent elsewhere (especially in Mulvey), the ascendancy of cultural studies, and in particular the Birmingham School, turned this capacity for resistance into a common reading strategy.

Central to socially-oriented questions of spectatorial agency was Stuart Hall's seminal thoughts on mass media interpretation in his 1973 article 'Encoding/decoding'. In it Hall made two important sets of distinctions.

Firstly, he addressed how meaning is encoded in a text by its producers, and decoded from the text by its consumers. Crucially, a gap exists between the two: what is encoded and what is decoded is different; there is no one-to-one correspondence between textual sign and, for example, spectatorial interpretation. Indeed, there are a variety of correspondences. Secondly, then, Hall would distinguish three kinds of reading positions: dominant, oppositional and negotiated. In the dominant reading of a text, readers accept what is encoded unproblematically and thus reinforce its ideological or *preferred* meaning. In the oppositional reading of a text, readers reject the dominant reading which is apparent but unacceptable to them owing to their social situation, and decode the text accordingly. In the negotiated reading both the dominant and oppositional readings have their appeals and decoding sits with and against the preferred reading (1980: 136–8). Of inside and outside, unfixed and open to contradiction, negotiated readings, unsurprisingly, would prove highly relevant to understandings of the female spectator. Indeed, as Christine Gledhill has argued, the representation of gender itself would become an obvious site of cultural negotiation during this time of 'active feminism, of social legislation for greater sexual equality and corresponding shifts in gender roles' (1988: 76).

It is worth noting that Hall's social semiotics corresponded with post-structuralism's meaning-liberation, discussed in chapter one. Where my 'soggy tissue/sad friend' scenario illustrated how the codes that determine our reading of signs power a chain of signification that allows us to read various levels of meaning, what is important now is how our response to these various levels is grounded in our lived social relations to the signs which direct or enable us to take or leave them. In other words, how I interpret and respond to my friend depends on my socially contextualised connection to her and her experience, and my capacity to act upon it (or personal confidence or chutzpah in doing so). So I might wholly accept what I see before me – my tearful dejected friend – as a pity-inspiring vision of personal misery and offer nothing but unconditional sympathy (a dominant reading). Alternatively, jaded by this the fifth romantic crisis of my love-junkie friend's year/appalled by her relentless pursuit of inappropriate partners/aware that we have completely different value systems and I never liked her much anyway, I decide to walk out and leave her to it (an oppositional reading). Or, finally, torn by the obviousness of her suffering but my lack of sympathy for her plight, I make her a cup of tea and tell her I can only stay for half an hour (a negotiated reading).

As attention shifted to the significance of social context in personalising cultural interpretation, so the agency of the individual as sign reader, now as cultural consumer, became ever more apparent. The Birmingham Centre for Contemporary Cultural Studies was at the forefront of this application of reception theory to mass media, or rather to its audiences, with David Morley's 1980 study of the reception of the British television programme *Nationwide* providing the formative case study.[9] According to Morley:

> Individuals in different positions in the social formation defined according to structures of class, race or sex, for example, will tend to inhabit or have at their disposal different codes and subcultures. Thus social position sets parameters to the range of potential readings by structuring access to different codes. (1983: 106–7)

Differences within and between social groups, then, become the key factor in determining their interpretation of mass culture. Gender was joined by a host of other permutations of identity in comprising the specificities of social formation. Audience studies became the primary method of accessing these specificities, and television the principle medium. Where cinema represented a rarefied space of regressive fantasies for an abstract spectator, television entered the home weaving the social realities of the small screen into the fabric of everyday life. Far from hypothetical, TV's in-the-flesh viewers glanced at and laughed at its realist tales, taking its characters at their word and with a pinch of salt. In other words, television offered a divergent landscape of representation for an oft-distracted but loyal, consistent but always varied, audience.

Television was also the logical focus of attention for feminist theorists of spectatorship. Here, after all, was a medium replete with 'gynocentric' narratives – those 'motivated by female desire and processes' (Kuhn 1992: 301) – and located in the woman's domain, one far from the darkness and stillness of the cinema auditorium. Comparisons between the subject positions on offer in film and television expanded feminists' field of vision. Television was also a medium hospitable to the mobility of its consumers: rooted as it is in the flexibility of its narratives, schedules, viewing patterns and, increasingly, formats. But, most importantly, as reception theory emphasised, television was predicated on the activity inherent in watching: you even had to turn the thing on yourself.

While the concern of this book lies not with television, the discussion of the activity and agency of the viewers looking on, and the model of reading positions that took hold during this period, instated key themes and conclusions about the agency of 'meaning making' for the continuing study of spectatorship. First, we might distinguish the over-simplification, and troubling autocracy, of the structuring of power through sexual difference: that male/female, active/passive polarity. The agency of the viewer-spectator, in inhabiting different viewing positions and decoding actively, was seen to be determined by more than gender. Rather than just acknowledging that differences existed between audience members, it became crucial to acknowledge how difference existed between women. As Charlotte Brundson put it in *Films for Women*, 'we may have biology in common, but the way in which we live out femininity is structured by class, ethnicity, sexual orientation, age, nationality, etc – and our understanding of these factors' (1986: 5).

The preoccupation with the singular differential of 'gender' – especially within 1970s feminist film theory – could be seen as masking other differences. More than this, it could inscribe its own exclusionary practices, its own disharmonious system, to function ideologically itself. As Mary Ann Doane and Janet Bergstrom clarified in the journal *Camera Obscura* in the special issue on the 'Spectatrix', cine-psychoanalysis was exposed as 'a primarily white, middle-class enterprise' (1989: 9). So it would seem that it was far more than a counter-cinema that was needed to escape the patriarchal prescriptions of classical Hollywood.

The female spectator, then, needed to be recognised for her multifarious social conditions, which, necessarily, confounded the generalisations of cine-psychoanalysis. These social conditions took into account the array of identity categories (though class and race would be the most vociferously explored: understandably so within the predominating US/UK axis of identity politics criticism). They also were required to be historically informed, as the work of both Tom Gunning (1989) and Miriam Hansen (1986; 1991) on early audiences argued. What these various explorations questioned was not just how the location of difference influenced which of the three ways of reading the spectator was likely to adopt but, crucially, that there was more to reading than these three modes. In other words dominant, oppositional and negotiated readings were not mutually exclusive. The key term in understanding this is 'pleasure', in particular how spectatorial pleasure operates beyond the scope of social formation. Oppositional pleasures could be taken from the 'dominant' text even as the preferred reading stays intact (so for example, *noir* could be enjoyed for its sadomasochistic fantasies without upsetting the conservative reading of narrative closure; more on this in chapter three.) At the same time, oppositional readings could replace one ideological discourse with another (so feminist film theory could be criticised, say, for rejecting sexism but reinforcing racism). Not to mention that what was being negotiated in a negotiated reading might have little to do with the either/or, the taking and leaving, of the texts' codes. In Jacqueline Bobo's (1988) application of Hall's theory to the reception of *The Color Purple* (1985), she argued that African-American women read not simply against the grain of the film, but beyond the film, to take pleasure in it. It is not that black female spectators acquiesced to a problematic production by a white man or to racist imag-ery (of black critics' focus) but that they chose not to let these interfere with the rare pleasure of a film's centralisation of black women's experiences.

Jane Gaines was also concerned with seeing how the pleasure of female spectators worked with or against not the text but critics' reading of it. In proposing women's 'alternative pleasures' in 1984, she reveals how 'women are daring to say that politically correct practices and proper fantasies do not necessarily fuel their passion … Restrained intellectual pursuits have a specialised recompense that bears little resemblance to the absorbing delight that means "pleasure" to so many women. Correct pleasure is a very privileged pleasure' (1990: 87). Not only is Gaines alluding to feminist theory's potential tyranny – how oppositional readings can come to pose as dominant fictions – but how pleasure can be incorrect: needing to be hidden; closeted. Homosexuality, in representing one set of socially-hidden pleasures, should be a key concern for spectatorship studies then: if feminist film theorists turned to the woman's film to challenge the 'classical' emphasis on the male-centred narrative, the lesbian spectator and/or lesbian film should provide an obvious focus for dispelling the heterosexual assumptions integral to Mulvey's model of spectatorship. That said, as Anneke Smelik illustrates, interest in lesbianism and lesbian and gay spectatorship was a long time coming (1999: 359–60).

What the focus on pleasure pointed to was the limitations of the social subject studied without reference to psychoanalysis, and of the capacity of its three associated modes of readings to work as catch-all terms for film's meaningfulness, for the machinations of social mores or for the spectator's contrariness or 'perversity' as Janet Staiger (2000) would call it. Spectatorial pleasure, or rather the passion, desires and fantasies that underpin it, evidences the prevalence and pull of illicit or unspoken or unconscious responses to film. So we must return, necessarily, to the influence of the psyche upon visual pleasure, while not letting go of the fact that visual pleasure, that fantasy, has 'never simply been a private affair' (Cowie 1997: 137). As spectatorship studies have continued to argue, in the realm of pleasure reception theory could only ever tell part of the story, or, as Jackie Stacey put it so well: 'it is only by combining theories of the psychic dimensions of cinematic spectatorship with analyses that are socially located that the full complexity of the pleasures of the cinema can be understood' (1994: 33). Indeed, Stacey's combined ethnographic and psychoanalytic approach to the study of female spectatorship in *Star Gazing* – as a convergence of the social and sexual, text and context – represented a crucial and timely example of that 'conjunctural' (Johnston 1992: 299), or 'context-activated' analyses (Staiger 1992: 59) that I prioritised in the introduction to this book. It is to this kind of convergence of approaches that we will aspire in the remaining chapters. Before we leave this schematic history of the theoretical relationship between spectatorship and difference via the tribulations of the female spectator, I want to take a brief look at what was going on for the male spectator during this period. While discussion of his social and psychic agency was an implicit, if necessarily marginalised, part of feminist developments within film and television criticism, in some of the key writings on masculinity and visual pleasure we find a recurrence of previous concerns and of those that will occupy us as we continue.

The male spectacle

If the female spectator could respond to the film text with not just activity but (voyeuristic) pleasure, what does this say about the male protagonist who, given the heterosexist/patriarchal economies of most films (and film criticism), must be rendered an object, a spectacle – that is feminised

– by default? And, if cinema provides us with male spectacles, what does this say about the male spectator who, given the dominance of his gaze, becomes (homo)erotically implicated?

In an influential article, Richard Dyer took on the thorny subject of the male object, by addressing his specific construction for the female consumer. Having acknowledged that women who look must do so surreptitiously, 'against the grain of their upbringing' (1982: 103) – providing a further permutation on oppositional readings – he turned his attention to the Male Pin-Ups aimed at a female audience. As sexual spectacles, the images seemed to violate the gendered codes of the gaze laid out so explicitly by Mulvey and John Berger (1972) before her, but they also contained various attempts to counteract this violation: to disavow their default passivity. Where a female model typically averts her eyes, out of modesty, patience, but certainly submission, the male model looks either up (contemplating higher things) or off (otherwise distracted) or, when he looks straight on, it is with the strong powerful stare of an equal or with a piercing gaze right through viewer. In other words, the male spectacle, while inevitably 'connoting *to-be-looked-at-ness*' (Mulvey 1992: 27), managed objectification in a specific, that is enduringly patriarchal, way. What is more, other differences were at stake in this management too: Dyer noted how ethnic and racial identity determined what kind of disavowing strategies were used.

Where Dyer introduced one set of disavowing strategies for how the 'still' image of the male dealt with its objectification, Steve Neale, in a piece in *Screen* the following year, revealed another set, and, more specifically, how the male spectacle in mainstream cinema 'managed' the homoeroticism inherent in the male spectator's objectifying gaze. There were always reasons – wholesome, virile, indisputably manly reasons – why the man would undress, would be frozen for a moment of erotic contemplation. Neale found that the display, and fetishisation, of the male body – that is, its construction for visual pleasure – in men's genres like the western, was accompanied by various, but distinctly male-centred, narratival displacements or licenses for that display, most commonly combat and its related actions. Such excuses for stilling the action, for exhibiting the male body, disavowed the implicated homoeroticism for 'the male body cannot be marked explicitly as the erotic object of another male look; that look must be motivated in some other way, its erotic component repressed' (1993:

14). Wounds, sport, self-sacrifice and so on comprised the growing list of excuses for male display, the disavowing strategies enabling the presentation of the objectified male (see Willemen 1981; Hunt 1993; Simpson 1994a; McKinnon 1999).

There are several crucial points to be drawn from this. First there is the ongoing centrality to spectatorship of the process of disavowal. Of increasing importance to my argument is how disavowal manages or contains the socially problematic, that is the 'perverse', implications of visual pleasure (rather than just the age-old anxieties of little boys). However, disavowal must not be seen as the preserve of the private, of psychic processes, but operates within public, social discourse as well. There is also the ongoing association of visual pleasure with masochism, originally noted of the heroines but now in holding out for the heroes too. The (homo)eroticism of the male spectacle is especially repressed but is still attached to the spectator's indulgence in his suffering. What Willemen called 'the unquiet pleasure of seeing the male mutilated' (1981: 16), connects with the sadomasochistic imaginary underpinning Rudolph Valentino's success (Hansen 1986) and the masochistic eroticism associated with male and female protagonists of classical Hollywood films like *Gilda* (Silverman 1983: 234) and of the Von Sternberg/Dietrich collaborations (Studlar 1988).

It is to these unquiet pleasures that I will now turn, in particular to the predicating of spectatorial pleasure upon the indulgence in the suffering of others. In the next chapter we will explore an alternative model of spectatorship, one grounded in masochism that takes into account the social and psychic management of the 'perverse' pleasures of spectatorship.

3   SPECTATORSHIP AS MASOCHISM: THE PLEASURE
OF UNPLEASURE

In the last chapter we explored feminist revisions to the classical model of
spectatorship. These revisions intervened at each level of its patriarchal
prescription to illustrate the female spectator's productivity, specificity or
powers of resistance, as well as the homoeroticism that underpins the male
spectator's visual pleasure. Despite the shift of attention to a live spectator, in all her polymorphous veracity, these interventions threw a certain
fuzziness over the issue of agency, echoing the post-structuralist project
and its eternal (if not infernal) deferral of meaning. The spectator became
so active a reader, that activity lost its agentic charge, it ceased to be the
obvious marker of autonomous act but became, instead, an inevitable if
not reflex reaction to the ever-proliferating and intersecting sets of signs
and ways of reading them. While the abstract spectator of the classical
model lacked agency in his or her virtuality (hardly surprising, given that
he was a product of illusion), so too does this *always atypical* spectator
of context-based criticism. This chapter seeks a compromise between the
nothing or all of these two positions, a theory of spectatorship that navi-
gates the former's inertia and the latter's ubiquity. As we move through the
second part of the book, the issue of agency gains in prominence as we
recognise its complexity within the negotiation of these opposing critical
positions, and evaluate its implications for contemporary 'real' spectatorial
experience. So at the same time as identifying the spectator's agency in
making active choices that cater to specific desires that are both inscribed
in and incited by the text, we must position these desires and choices as
socio-historically meaningful.

Laura Mulvey's theories of spectatorship saw classical cinema as sadistic, as an institution that inflicts and allows to dominate, if not to triumph, the gaze of the aggressor. Film's sadism, its 'doing to' the spectator against 'his' will, might be *resisted*, the prominent description of a notional spectatorial agency that opposes submissiveness, but resistance still sustains the structure of binary logic and, because of the discourses that this structure holds up, its implicit oppression. As long as this classical system remained intact, then, as the governing grid of interpretation, so too would the ideological (the sexist and heterosexist) system that it codified. Indeed, as French feminist philosophers argued at the time, the problem was precisely the binary logic of phallocentrism, rather than simply phallocentrism itself (see Cixous 1981). Our attention turns then to a counter-model of spectatorship, to exploring the activity of the spectator and rethinking its social implications. Where chapter two challenged the equation of agency and masculinity through a focus on gender, here we question the equation of agency with activity, through a focus on masochism.

Simply stated, masochism is the pleasure of unpleasure, it is an active desire played out through passivity. In its complexity, in its critical heritage and cultural currency, masochism affords remarkable insight not only into spectatorship but contemporary film culture. Reading spectatorship as masochistic is, I would suggest, unavoidable for it provides the most compelling description of the pleasures offered by, and met through, the film text, but there are many other benefits to privileging masochism. For Steven Shaviro, an early advocate, masochism's alternative scheme privileged ambivalent pleasures over both the monogamy of spectatorial identification and the Freudian binarisms underlying it (1993: 59). Most importantly, then, masochism moves on from the inadequacies of (cine)psychoanalysis. It does this both through bridging the active versus passive divide and instating social context and through its critical evolution which breaks with Freudian conservatism to distinguish the cultural masochism underwriting our contemporary relations to art.

What is more, in emphasising not only the agency inherent in submission but submission's contractual core, masochism affords a pursuit of an ethics of spectatorship that forms the focus of the final chapter. Let us begin by tracing a path through the critical evolution of masochism from and after Freud, to reveal its emerging characteristics and how they are so applicable to cinema and spectatorship.

Mapping human function and dysfunction within child development and adult socialisation, was, for Freud, crucial both as scientific intervention and therapeutic tool. His emphases upon neuroses not only revealed the machinations of the mind but, crucially, paved the routes to psychological cure. However, Freud was increasingly troubled by the illogic of individuals' resistance to getting better, to ridding themselves of 'unpleasure', as he put it. In various essays in the early 1900s, Freud tried to figure out why patients specifically and humans in general endured and even enjoyed discomfort. Why do we grin and bear it?

What he came up with were various conclusions about masochism. These broadened its existing definition as a perverse form of sexual pleasure – caused by being inflicted with, or anticipating, pain – to account for masochism's desexualised presence as a toleration or even indulgence in 'unpleasure'. These various conclusions represented important developments in his thinking on the subject during this period. These developments revolved mainly around a 'chicken or egg'-like reckoning over which came first, which dominates, sadism or masochism? A similar question – of whether cinema, and by extension, culture, operates through a sadistic (as Mulvey-esque feminist theory would have it) or a masochistic economy – underlies this chapter of the book, and the relationship between the two will prove crucial to the discussion as it unfolds. But let us stick with Freud for the time being, who in exploring and ultimately privileging masochism elucidated its main characteristics; characteristics that prove increasingly useful for our understanding of our relationship to the world, and to our evolving discussion of film spectatorship.

The central point about Freud's emerging theory of masochism was its conservatism. On a basic level, this is instantly readable via the 'patriarchal unconscious' of psychoanalysis mentioned in the last chapter: the ready association of the negativity of masochism with the weaknesses of femininity. Indeed, Freud's most conservative or misogynistic form of masochism, feminine masochism, was also, according to him, the 'most accessible to our observation and least problematical' (1991b: 416). In this way, Freudian masochism has been interpreted, retroactively, as inherently conservative in its working for the patriarchal project. But Freud himself saw masochism as implicitly conservative too, in that it served the status quo.

Both his claims about masochism's function – that it operated as a temporary pathology or perverse pleasure and that it represented the most fundamental human instinct – revealed its goal as serving the self-strengthening
principle that underwrites our sometimes self-destructive behaviours. It is
this sense of its conservatism that we shall pursue further.

Freud distinguished various moments where the individual indulged
'his' own suffering. The neurotic's therapeutic experience provided one,
smallish, set of such moments. Here, for example, an individual could
disrupt cure through repression or transference: could replenish past
trauma either by holding back, rather than letting out, important emotions,
or by projecting them onto the therapist. But most masochism, for Freud,
arose within compulsive repetition, within the individual's insistent revis-
iting of unpleasurable feelings. Freud initially located this indulgence in
suffering in terms of war or traumatic neuroses where, for example, the
ex-soldier revisits his disturbing experience during dreaming. Though he
keeps returning to the site and experience of 'unpleasure', this masochistic
tendency must be thought of as only temporary: neurotic activity that can
be overcome through therapy.

The other site for Freud's continuing investigation of compulsive repetition is the *fort/da* game, and with it comes the initial inklings of the nature
of masochistic pleasure, pleasure as deferred and thereby exceeding his
existing ideas about the pleasure principle and its stake in immediacy
(Freud 1991a: 281–7). In the *fort/da* game the infant re-creates the departure and reappearance of 'his' mother – her absence as 'gone' (*fort*) and
presence as 'there' (*da*). Freud both locates and quantifies the pleasure
within the unpleasurable scenario:

> The child cannot possibly have felt his mother's departure as some-
> thing agreeable or even indifferent. How then does his repetition of
> this distressing experience as a game fit in with the pleasure prin-
> ciple? It may perhaps be said in reply that her departure had to be
> enacted as a necessary preliminary to her joyful return, and that
> it was in the latter that lay the true purpose of the game. (1991a:
> 285)

What Freud suggests is that the pleasure of recovery is not only experienced
through the pain of loss, but is actually *increased* by it. The unpleasure is

temporary and necessary for the greater pleasure to be experienced; it is an essential part of the achievement of joy. This is a crucial point, confirming a conservative paradigm for this behaviour: the indulgence in loss for the enhancement of the later gain.

The conservatism of this game also existed within its function as an episode of mastery.[1] The child pre-empts displeasure, staging sadness and joy before they are imposed upon 'him'. The child enacts control of an otherwise helpless situation; he actively, and even vengefully, anticipates 'what might be feared to occur to one passively', as Rudolph M. Loewenstein put it (1995: 37). The child gets there first. As such, the masochistic practice affords the individual a degree of agency within his submission to fate. This is crucial: that even here, with Freud for whom masochism was a decidedly powerless or negative stake or state, we find masochism's complicated relationship to activity. This is really why I am dwelling on Freud, despite the clear cut anti-Freudian privileging of masochism as pleasure that directs my argument later.

As well as affording these episodes of mastery, masochism contributed to the smooth running of a far more fundamental process, according to Freud. While such external practices as mastery served the life instincts, these were not the primary instincts. Instead, the 'primordial force' was the Death Instinct and, as Jean Laplanche clarifies, 'every living being aspires to death by virtue of its most fundamental *internal* tendency' (1976: 107). Thus Eros, the pleasure principle or Life Instinct, is joined by Thanatos, the Death Instinct. Freud would come to show how the two instincts work together, but their ultimate aim is the return to 'an earlier state of things', the inorganic, the dead (1991a: 308). The primacy of the life instincts – of self-preservation, self-assertion and mastery – recedes. They serve the Death Instinct, merely defending against the 'unnatural' disruption (or, rather, fulfilment) of the Death Instinct.

> Hence arises the paradoxical situation that the living organism struggles most energetically against events (dangers, in fact) which might help it to attain its life's aim rapidly – by a kind of short-circuit. (1991a: 311–12)

These events or dangers become overdetermined with the heightened struggle against them. As in the *fort/da* game, they could be seen as the necessary precursors to a greater joy. These dangers need to be indulged that they can be surpassed for greater reward. The dangerous events, the self-imposed or externally enforced obstacles to life, oppose the death drive. Yet their challenge to it is necessary, it seems, for the efficacious functioning of the system, which is not content merely to seek death but to perpetuate life until the natural and almost pre-programmed attainment of the inevitable. In this way the self-endangering act is, thus, a *necessary* obstacle to the Death Instinct: in constantly testing itself the death drive would seem to be hardened in its resolve.

So, according to Freud, individuals subject themselves to things 'not nice' in order to enhance the pleasure, and other benefits, felt when it is over. They also engage in masochistic events or dangers in order to elaborately stage or test their own resolve, or will to survival, to fulfil their destiny or, at least, to have a keener sense of it. It is easy to see why some theorists would look to the arts as a site which provides episodes of mastery or fortifying tests to the death drive, and is an intrinsically safe site at that in being premised upon vicarious rather than 'live' experience. Loewenstein, for example, suggests that danger-filled genres cater to this precisely: 'gruesome fairytales, thrillers, mystery plays and horror films seem to be an institutionalised means of gratifying the same [psychic] need' (1995: 37). Ernest Becker (1973) wrote of the representation of masochism in visual culture in similar terms, as a social denial of death through the distillation of the anxieties surrounding it. Cinema certainly provides 'not nice' experiences: when we share the protagonist's horror at his new wife's death, we despair at a distance in the knowledge that it is not our loss but his. It also stages masochistic events or dangers: when we watch Tom Cruise dangling from a broken cord on the sheer face of a cold mountain, we struggle to avoid death even if at one remove. In other words, it is easy to see how film affords these conservative masochistic episodes that serve to strengthen the spectator's subjectivity, to heighten the sense of our own survival. But are these episodes, and the pleasures they offer, always contained so neatly within the narrative? Does masochism only operate through isolated events for the characters or for the spectators? And is it always so conservative, or patriarchal, in its purposefulness?

To begin to answer these questions we must move on from Freudian understandings of masochism as psychic (mal)function and pursue its status as a culturally acknowledged and culturally performed pleasure in its own right. In being gratuitous, its sexual component, which Freud saw as 'never far away' from its desexualised practices anyhow, becomes ever more conspicuous. That is not to say that in claiming masochism as pleasure, or as cultural, one does not dally with its psychological causes. In fact, psychoanalytic theory underlies such claims, albeit in an anti-Freudian emphasis upon the masochism of the pre-Oedipal stage, rather than the sadism of the Oedipal (a distinction that will become clear later). At the same time, masochism has not, for various reasons – several lucrative – shaken off its ties to sexual deviancy. But its pervasive indulgence within culture testifies primarily to the masses' masochistic preferences to which it necessarily caters. In other words, cultural masochism represents a cultural desire. Whether as the individual's desire that is fed by culture or is created by culture in directing the formation of taste, pleasure in an indulgence in, or identification with, suffering underwrites the appeal of much of our arts entertainment and other media forms. This is not news (although it is true of the news). According to Nick Mansfield masochism 'exists at the intersection and overlap of a whole set of personal sexual practices, on the one hand, and public cultural ones, on the other hand' (1997: xii). Let us see, then, how these intersect and overlap in the realm of cinema, how masochism resonates within our discussion of film spectatorship.

The pleasure of unpleasure

Masochism's main presence within film theory had lain within the discussion of melodramas of the 1940s and 1950s and their whimpering heroines whose tragic fates epitomised the propensity both of women – as characters and as spectators – to 'choose' suffering, and of cinema to perpetuate, sadistically of course, this patriarchally expedient preference. The much written about *Letter from an Unknown Woman* (1948) provides the quintessential example of this kind of female masochistic passage, but – and this is crucial – it also evidences the more pervasive and persuasive presence of masochistic pleasure. It is not that its sane but self-sacrificing heroine Lisa (Joan Fontaine) breaks the mould of the ill-fated female, but that, as Gaylyn Studlar (1994) has suggested, this mould is both more complex and more broadly implicating than feminist responses to the women's film had, albeit necessarily, allowed for.

In *Letter from an Unknown Woman* Lisa selects a path through life characterised by submission, suffering and sacrifice. An adolescent obsession with the compulsively forgetful womaniser Stefan (Louis Jourdan) comes to shape her adulthood of unrequited but unconditional love for him, at a distance, manifested as repeated disappointment and, finally, death after she falls victim to the same disease that claimed their son. All this is revealed in a letter to the otherwise oblivious Stefan, opened by him at the start of the film and enacted, as flashback, as the film's story.

Though Lisa seems to epitomise the masochistic heroine of Mary Ann Doane's formulation, there is little that is weak or emotionally fragile, that is, pathologically feminine, about her. Instead, as Lucy Fischer clarifies, she is sane and stoic (1990: 172). Lisa exerts a remarkable level-headedness during even her most illogical acts. For Fischer, this is proof of the social rather than psychic platform upon which female masochism is played out within men and women's different stakes in romance: so that Lisa is self-punishing devotee to Stefan the womaniser. In connecting Lisa's romantic dedication to a feminine perpetuation of suffering, Fischer, in line with Doane, denies Lisa any pleasure in this position, and thoroughly de-sexualises her. However, like Studlar, I find this reading far from compelling, for it is the ecstasy of Lisa's abiding but distant desire for Stefan that haunts and dictates all her future actions. 'And though you didn't know it' she writes to him, 'you were giving me some of the happiest hours of my life.' It is the always present/always potential return of the rapturous joy of his attention that premises Lisa's choices and fuels her endless wait. What could be a more convincing tract on masochistic pleasure than this?

Instead of seeing the film, then, as repeating the familiar fable of female victimisation, Studlar exposed Lisa as the active and desiring agent of her own fantasy-fuelled choices. These choices demarcate a distance from and deferral of pleasure – Lisa favours waiting over having – and they are staged, and overvalued, within a devout display of self-sacrifice. Rather than simply and silently submitting to her victim status, Lisa invites this role through her various wound-enhancing, healing-avoidance behaviours. She watches Stefan, even with other women, she resists her own recovery, she suspends her life within an aura of erotic fixation, and she does so willingly and wittingly with eyes both wide and bright. Leaving Linz, and her mother, to dedicate herself to her obsessive love, she returns 'night after night ... to the same spot' outside his home in Vienna, until one evening Stefan does

Fig. 4 *Letter from an Unknown Woman*: Lisa'a masochistic longing

notice her, and they embark on a brief affair. Heading to the fairground that night, Stefan remarks how he prefers it off season, that the place is 'more pleasant in the winter, I don't know why'. Lisa, of course, knows why: 'It is perhaps because you prefer to imagine how it will be in the spring. Because if it is spring then there is nothing to imagine.' She immediately locates the pleasure of such a preference: the masochistic favouring of anticipation over apprehension. Similarly, the religious iconography punctuating the narrative – the convent and nuns she goes to for the delivery of her baby, the cross-embossed paper she uses for the letter – lends not, as Fischer would have it, an appropriately sacred air to Lisa's romantic idealisation of Stefan. Rather, it seasons the story with the high art of masochistic aesthetics: ascetic ritual and its primary signifier, Christ. That the film self-consciously *enacts* Lisa's story, bringing her letter to life as it were, furthers the sense of a dramatisation of masochistic pleasure, and, of course, one that is distinctly catering to those looking on, to the spectators.

    Lisa's choices, and the narrative which stages them, are oriented towards masochism: masochism not as a perverse investment in feeling pain, as Freudian feminists would have it, but as a 'perverse' pleasure in indulging in a fantasy of, that is not actual, pain. This latter conceptualisation is drawn from Gilles Deleuze's radical reconsideration of Freudian masochism (via Theodor Reik's revisions (1941)), and underlies Studlar's groundbreaking work that applies it to cinema, and reclassifies spectatorship (1985). Central to this conceptualisation was the distinction of several key qualities of masochism. Instead of emphasising the conservative/Freudian logic of the happy ending – cure, self-fortification, mastery – Deleuze offered an alternative reading of compulsive repetition and the *fort/da* game in which he privileged the process of waiting. Masochism, he states, is 'waiting in its pure form' (1991: 71). Rather than pleasure being achieved and enhanced by the wait being over (read: the desired object is relished all the more because it was such a long time coming), pleasure is heightened through anticipation itself (excitement grows with expectation of the desired object's arrival ... having it could only be disappointing). For Deleuze, then, waiting is gratuitous: 'The masochist waits for pleasure as something that is bound to be late ... He therefore postpones [it] in expectation of the pain which will make gratification possible' (ibid.). This sense of the pleasures inherent in waiting, in postponement, clearly resonates within the dramatic strategies of narrative entertainment, especially suspense.

Masochistic pleasure is also to be characterised by a fantasy of pain. In *Masochism in Modern Man*, Reik introduced masochism as the desire for the idea of pain rather than its actuality. 'Masochism is not, as has been surmised up till now, characterised by the pleasure in discomfort, but by pleasure in the *expectation* of discomfort' (1941: 67). Distanced from Freud, Reik began to explore this more transgressive permutation of masochism as about the idea, the performance of suffering. Most importantly, how masochism is not simply 'active' as a desire but that it is a disavowal of activity, a disavowal that is enacted through or evidenced by this contrived staging of a pained prolonging. While Freud wrestled with a certain activity of masochism, a sense of masochistic mastery, masochism remains a more complicated submission than he afforded, with the masochist's control inscribed on every level of 'his' submission. Where Freud posited the masochist as passive, Reik and then Deleuze thoroughly rejected the passivity of 'his' position: the masochist's misery was, for most intents and purposes, for show. As with exhibitionism, which Reik linked it to, control is inherent within passivity: 'the showing or wanting-to-be-seen is actually a means to invite the sexually gratifying punishment' (1941: 73). This emphasis upon display or staging within masochism isolates yet another dramatic strategy, and a further inherent affinity between masochism and cinema.

A crucial additional point to the masochist's activity in summoning the other party's cruel treatment is that the other party is to be distinguished as additional performer in this masochistic scenario, and not, as Freud and Freudian feminists would have it, as a sadist. Masochists are not the passive halves in the charmed coincidence of a sadist-masochist meeting, but have fundamentally opposing agendas. The masochist does not legitimise sadism, but wants a sadist as little as a sadist requires or desires a masochist. The sadist's source of pleasure, according to Deleuze's reading of the Marquis de Sade, is the very absence of voluntariness. The masochist, then, as willing victim is excluded from the sadist's wish-list (1991: 40–1). The extraneous object for the masochist's scheme is the antithesis of a sadist: a persuaded and encouraged actor of purely 'fictitious power': a pseudo-sadist (Smirnoff 1995: 69). Of course, in the realm of cinema sadists, that is, screen sadists, are always only invested with fictitious power. So the masochist requires another party for the fulfilment of his or her scheme, 'he' requires 'witnesses to his pain and degradation' (Reik 1941: 136). *Letter from an Unknown Woman* makes such witnesses of us all: Lisa sets her suffering out for Stefan to read and as such regales us with her pitiful plight. Stefan is far from fiendish: he is neither harsh nor heartless in his encounters or words. In fact, the opposite is true: when he gives Lisa his attention it is full and loving. 'Promise me you won't vanish' he says to her, and, right after, must track her down to her place of work: 'how did you find me?' she asks. Stefan's flaw, as has been documented, is his narcissism, his inability to move beyond his selfish, immediate needs (Studlar 1994: 46). Yet this manifests itself through many of the same tropes as the masochist's, through thwarted ambition and compulsive repetitions, deferral and waiting. When the pair meet again by chance at the opera some nine years on, Lisa, having heard others refer to Stefan's fall from glory and he himself state that he no longer plays piano, asks him about it: 'I always tell myself I'll begin again next week and then when next week is this week, I wait for next week again.' He, too, is trapped in a cycle of self-limiting behaviours that sees him fail in love and life. Indeed, the film ends (as it began) with reference to Stefan's imminent duel. A masochistic economy underwrites the masochistic text and the behaviours of all its participants, even in their pseudo-sadism. Masochism in its strange position between activity and passivity, between pain and pleasure, between submission and control, inscribes a world in which the spectator as witness is similarly strangely positioned but always, as will become increasingly significant, complicit.

Reik delineated several principles of masochism, then, that hinged upon its activity, or rather the activity inherent in submission. These principles were fantasy, suspense and the demonstrative or, as Deleuze more usefully puts it, the persuasive. Masochistic pleasure is not self-contained; it relies upon the cruel-ness of strangers, as it were, *but* it both distinguishes and encourages them in this role, thoroughly distinguishing them, therefore, from 'true' sadists. To Reik's list, Deleuze adds the provocative, that 'the masochist aggressively demands punishment' (1991: 75). He also notes the absence of a fifth factor, which is the contract, a factor that is central to his thesis and to my next and final chapter, but for now further suggests the agency of the masochist despite appearances. The masochist is a strange wallflower: a more than willing witness to 'his' own ruination, sitting out, spectator only, to a dance 'he' choreographed. For Studlar this activity-in-passivity, or activity-as-passivity combination, which defines the masochist, plays out in film through the centrality of a 'perverse masquerade', a stylised performance of seemingly unwelcome suffering, a self-rendering 'as done to'. In it Lisa 'is eager to bear witness to her own victimised status and to exploit the technique of confession in bringing her seemingly "innocent" fantasies to light' (1994: 41). This masquerade 'uncannily corresponds to Deleuze's description of the masochistic text that constructs a persuasively perverse heterocosm in which the apparent victim speaks a deceptive discourse masking the true hierarchy of desire' (ibid.). In this true hierarchy of desire, the masochist runs the show. He/she is the one 'controlling the other's control' (L. R. Williams 1989: 14). The lady must protest too much, that the perverse pleasure she takes in her powerlessness is not exposed, for to expose it would run the risk not only of ending it but of revealing the perversity of the entire scenario, and this is classical cinema after all.

But something is missing; too implicit to my argument when it needs to be made explicit. In each of these steps, from the bearing witness, to the technique of confession, to the emphasis upon performance, the allusion to, metaphor for, and downright summoning of the spectator is striking. Who, after all, is this dramatisation of masochistic pleasure for? Who 'pays for' the suspense, the fantasy of pain, the disavowal of activity? Who looks on in rapt attention, seated, silenced, watching the overtly dramatic strategies play out? There is a remarkable convergence of the spectator's and Lisa's position: through the masochistic pleasure of our sacrificial heroine we can better see the masochistic pleasure of the film spectator, as each submits, willingly, to the unfolding but not unexpected story. But this discussion does not mean to replicate recurring flaws of film theory in arguing either that the spectator's experience is determined by the central character with whom one categorically identifies, or, alternatively, that films are most interesting, or telling, when they work as metaphors for spectatorship. Instead, in favouring the terms 'masochistic economy' or 'masochistic orientation' over the 'masochistic text' (Deleuze) or 'masochistic aesthetic' (Studlar), masochism is instated as operating on a variety of levels. It is not just a set of acts or inclinations but represents the fabric, and fuelling, of the film. Most importantly, it is intersubjective: always about a dynamic with others, a dynamic of expectation and delight that connects the individual in the audience with the character on screen. Studlar's distinction of two forms of cinematic masochism, the textual and the psychic, has provided a solid but flawed foundation for our evolving discussion (1988: 9). While we will continue to pursue the aesthetic, narrative and psychological strategies that constitute the masochism of spectatorship, the ahistoricism of her approach will become ever less tenable. So too does the persistence of the perversity of masochism, which, despite her broadening her remit in turning to the woman's film to find women masochistically pleasured too, Studlar continues to leave intact (see L. R. Williams 1989: 205).

What I hope to have shown is that *Letter from an Unknown Woman* in particular, like melodrama in general, enacts and invites masochistic pleasures both on- and off-screen. Indeed, the genre depends upon spectatorship's masochistic orientation. However, to discern the spectator's 'pleasure' in watching these films is, it must be said, a tricky thing to do not least because of melodrama's relative sobriety, but also because we must, surely, have some compelling sense of the parameters for the creation and discernment of pleasure. (And smile counting at the cinema, cue computing from the text, or reifying audience questionnaires, are, in my view at least, illusory gauges of such things.) Let us turn, then, to something more explicitly intoxicating and twisted, to a kind of film that draws its tone, punch and popularity from the incitement and inscription of pleasures that are distinctly disagreeable *and* exciting in essence, to film noir and its contemporary form, the erotic thriller.

Noir and masochism

As another genre or mode of films that is often discussed in terms of its protagonist's self-destructiveness, *noir* provides an important focus of attention here for several reasons. Firstly, and most importantly, its steady heady mixing of the sexy and the dangerous make it the mainstream's most explicit exploitation of the pleasures of unpleasure. Secondly, it has provided a playground for many a film theorist bent on furthering our understanding of the connections between American social history, film style and cinema's sexual politics. For Laura Mulvey, for example, its femme fatale was the embodiment of patriarchal anxieties, and *noir* became the case study of choice for illustrating the classical model of spectatorship. As such it is an apposite site to test out and instate an opposing model. Thirdly, in its endurance and evolution within film history, predominantly via the sexualisation of its central couple, it casts cultural and historical perspective onto cinema's play upon, and popularisation of, perversity. Fourth, the erotic power dynamic between the films' couples and the textual play upon watching, waiting and fantasising, intensifies, and not only analogously, the spectatorial process. Let us begin by casting previously distinguished characteristics of the masochistic text or aesthetic upon classical *noir* in order to expand their realm of influence and, ultimately, question masochism's continuing currency as a model of spectatorship.

Film noir has been beset with problems of definition, but of the raw materials contributing to its categorisation as a genre – its cinematic flagrancy, narrative structure, moribund fascinations – the *noir* quality I want to focus on is the erotic dynamic between the two key characters.[2] This dynamic is premised on the danger of their liaison, a danger that arises not simply in its association with breaking the law but with the immanence of suffering or of death that haunts and fuels their relationship and the narrative itself. The protagonists' erotic quests are framed by inevitability, both in terms of unrealisable ambition but also their, predominantly common, demise. In such typical *noirs* as *Double Indemnity*, *Out of the Past* and *The Killers* both protagonists die. Despite critics' frequent polarisation of the evil manipulative woman and abused good guy (who, like the heroine of the melodrama, is perversely, that is conservatively, masochistic precisely through his feminine vulnerability and fatefulness), the two are comparable and compatible in their desires and destiny. They choose their fates, follow their hearts or hard-ons and, for the fall guy most prominently, do so in a manner characterised by tropes of victimisation (entrapment, torment, ruination). They act out these choices in an oddly elaborate way, so that a masochistic ethos is not only encoded within film style and structuring – iconography, repetitive narrative, oscillating emotions – but is also actually articulated, albeit understatedly, throughout. As such it always references the performance of the perversion, and an active one of that. For example, the following striking sample of dialogue, from the central couple's first meeting in *Double Indemnity*, is intoned with the disinterest of deadpan banter and infused with a well-crafted vying for power.

Walter: Suppose you get down off your motorcycle and give me
          a ticket.
Phyllis: Suppose I let you off with a warning this time.
Walter: Suppose it doesn't take.
Phyllis: Suppose I have to whack you over the knuckles.
Walter: Suppose I bust out crying and put my head on your
          shoulder.

Based upon his provocation of her threatened punishments within what could only be described as fantasy role-play (he as naughty driver, she as cruel cop), this first flirtation is underwritten by masochism. It is also prophetic of the entire film, not simply through their ongoing dynamic (she as cold and comforting, he as demonstrative and demanding) but also through Walter's bidding to break the law, and through the presaging of the possibility of him taking the rap.

The stock figure of the *noir* world is the man who falls for and pursues the cruel temptress and is locked, thereafter, into the masochistic pleasure of prospective pain that this fixation, with the guarantor of his demise, inspires. He is attracted to the dangerousness she represents; he is told the water is probably scalding but dives in regardless. While Elizabeth Cowie suggests that 'it is precisely her dangerous sexuality that he desires, so that it is ultimately his own perverse desire that is his downfall' (1993: 125), let me clarify that it is ultimately his downfall that is his perverse desire. I say this not to reinstate the primacy of the death wish or some other recuperative tendency in our middle management of mortality. No, this clarification fully frames the pleasure of spectatorship within the fantasy of death, that is, within the always absent actual death for the spectator that film, and especially these films, afford. In other words, death hovers in the protagonists' future in the film but never ours. What is more, Walter's flirtation with defying the law, with risking his own downfall, operates outside of Phyllis's incitement or threatened punishments: he speaks of his pre-existing desire to beat the system by making the perfect criminal insurance claim. Phyllis provides him with the opportunity for wish-fulfillment as much as he does her. The *noir* man will risk all, or, like Walter, will represent All Risk – the insurance company Walter works for. That its complete title is Pacific All Risk, provides a neat, and again announced, encapsulation of the dialectic of masochism, its marriage of seeming opposites in combining the one who will never 'step up' with the one who always will. The notion of a calm-claiming thrill-seeker represents a provocative disavowal of activity indeed, and one that is laboured for (and often by) the spectator specifically, through the repetition of the company's name in dialogue – 'all what?' Phyllis asks, when Walter announces his affiliation – and in close-ups of its inscription.

The *noir* couple's dynamic is characterised by masochism alone for other, archetypal, reasons too. Like the pre-Oedipal mother – who both gives into and denies the child, indulges and disciplines, is there (*fort*) and gone (*da*) – the femme fatale blows hot and cold, and the couple's relationship is characterised by this masochistic oscillation. Sometimes she is loving, sometimes cruel. Kathy in *Out of the Past* will give herself to Jeff, then later run out on him after she shoots their pursuer, leaving him with the body. When they meet again she will declare that she never stopped loving him; that she had to leave and had to betray him. Jeff waits for her next appearance, her next embrace or rejection of him. His hard-boiled rhetoric is, as in *Double Indemnity*, an implausible performance of disinterest. He will tell his new girlfriend he feels nothing for Kathy any more, he will exude cool and control when he sees Kathy again, but within moments she is in his arms and he is devising their escape. He keeps making the same mistake again, not because he does not know what she is like, but because he does. We are far from surprised by his failure to move on: what could conjure the going-nowhereness of the masochist better than the garage or gas station owner – the dupes' jobs in *Out of the Past* and *The Killers* – whose stasis is striking through their contrast to the other drivers.

The man is not simply a dupe, and neither is the woman simply a vamp. She is set up as nothing but trouble often before we meet her: there are repeated warnings about Kitty in *The Killers* and Kathy in *Out of the Past*. Should our meeting be a long time coming – and given her often symbolic/ peripheral status it often is – we surmise her guilt from the broken, faded or fading male figure who initiates the narrative: the injured, sweating Walter; the reclining, still and sad Swede awaiting his executioners in the dark. Of course our ability to surmise this is grounded in distinct sign-readings on the part of the spectator. By this sign-reading I mean how the spectator's projection is based both upon the obligatory romance plot, or its sexist logic that 'puts the blame on Mame', and upon a recognition of narrative trajectory borne of familiarity with the genre or mode, and with the stars of the film even, or especially, when they are acting against type. In other words, we must also always acknowledge the foreknowledge and pre-sell of the genre film. As Richard Maltby put it: 'We know a thriller when we see one. Indeed, we know a thriller before we see one' (1995: 107). Let us not forget, though, that the classification of *noir* as genre has been both messy and retroactive, and as such delimits the foreknowledge of its contemporaneous spectator. While spectatorial 'knowingness' becomes increasingly indisputable over time (as the erotic thriller evolves, as film culture diversifies and dominates leisure activities, and as the contemporary spectator watches classical *noir*), it still plays an important part in an anticipatory mode of spectatorship invited by film structure and content, a point I will return to below.

In recasting *noir* as masochistic text, the femme fatale can escape her reductive definition as symptom or catch phrase of patriarchal fear, or as sadist, and be acknowledged as the complex character she often is in these films (Bronfen 2004). Not only does she sometimes voice the inevitability of her own demise, or reveal some home-truths about her admirer, but she also frequently equates the two of them. In doing so she confirms their compatibility but, more importantly, the common – that is masochistic – economy underwriting the pseudo-sadist/victim pairing and the films themselves. *Gilda*, for example, provides one of cinema's most famous and least straightforward femmes fatale. Rita Hayworth's eponymous heroine manipulates and is manipulated, brandishes bravado and sincerity in equal measure. She tantalises the audience, both inside and outside the film, with her musical numbers and general prowess, and displays both vulnerability and canniness. Phyllis in *Double Indemnity* is explicit about the sameness of her and Walter; they are as guilty as each other she claims, and they are both 'in it together straight down the line' to the end. Likewise, Kathy in *Out of the Past* says of herself and Jeff that they 'are both rotten'.

Critics' interest in the femme's fatal-ness rather than her fatalism – what she represents for men rather than what she represents for herself and other women – favours her role as guarantor of the perverse appeals of the dupe's imminent suffering. But she is often implicated in this masochistic narrative as much as he is. Their shared demise and the air of inevitability pervading the films do not so much elevate her dangerousness as prove the self-fulfilling, masochistic logic of their relationship. Within the 'sadomasochism' of the couple's dynamic – for both submissive and aggressive acts are expressed even though, as I argue, they add up to masochis – the protagonists swing both ways. She is the threatening 'torturer' in the erotic role-play, intermittently source of comfort and cruelty. But he too can be cold and punishing. Indeed, Walter and Jeff will see the femmes killed in their final encounters. While the construction of beauty in the films might seem to fall squarely on setting up the female spectacle, so that Phyllis, Kathy and Kitty all enter the frame as *uber*-elevated objects of desire, the men are far from punters at the pageant. Burt Lancaster's sweaty musculinity in the boxing ring, his pout and puppy-like devotion is joined by Robert Mitchum's floppy hair and sleepy, come-from-bed eyes and manner. Even Walter enters as wise-guy and womaniser. In other words the reductive 'bad but beautiful woman hooks gullible guy' take on *noir* has masked (often for politically expedient reasons) the more complex play on power and submission, desire and destructiveness, accessed through spectatorship. So while gender continues to be a crucial factor in the interpretation of characterisations and categorisations, there is a lot more to it, as the discussion of the contemporary erotic thriller below will suggest.

That highly suggestive banter between Phyllis and Walter in *Double Indemnity* draws their first meeting to an end and follows on from Walter's first sight of Phyllis, which initiated the sexual terms of their encounter within the classical terrain of the voyeuristic-exhibitionistic axis of spectatorship. Walter enters the Dietrichson household to pitch insurance policies and Phyllis, asking her housekeeper who it is, looks down from the first floor landing with just a towel wrapped around her. Walter then waits excitedly in the drawing room for a 'decent' Phyllis to descend. Her descent has the camera dwelling, in close-up, on her anklet in a move that

Fig. 5 *Double Indemnity*: 'that's a honey of an anklet you're wearing...'

many have focused on for its encapsulation of the fetishistic process. That is, that the power that Phyllis embodies is immediately managed, for and by the male gaze, through the fragmentation and overvaluation of the body part. Moving away from this, Elizabeth Bronfen (2004) reads the scene not as simply alleviating male anxiety but as acknowledging the refusal of Walter to 'see' Phyllis, in a manner in which throughout the film Phyllis will demand to be seen. I want to argue, however, that this scene, despite its conventional yet various appeals to feminist film theory, clearly constructs a masochistic position for, and caters to the masochistic pleasure of, the spectator. Phyllis is no simple spectacle: this is not your classical exhibitionism, which enables but disavows voyeurism in a casual causality. She positively wants to be looked at, and looked at indecently: she steps forward with only a towel wrapped around her, she enters the drawing room still buttoning up her shirt. Those witnessing this are not sneaking a look, they are catching what is thrown at them. The fetish is not about dispelling male fears about female power: this is not your classical disavowal of castration. The fetish does not stand in for the lost phallus in line with the traditional feminist story of the male-identified gaze. No, instead the fetish, like *noir* itself, is about painful pleasure: it is about an indulgence in (displaced) fear or pain in anticipation of an always-later comfort. It represents the pain of separation, standing in for *da* lost mother. In other words, this key moment of fetishism is resolutely connected to masochism, of the pre-Oedipal phase, and not to sadism, of the Oedipal phase.

This all important distinction of *Double Indemnity*'s masochistic orientation is compounded by Walter's later comment in voice-over: 'I kept thinking of Phyllis Dietrichson and the way that anklet of hers cut into her leg.' An eroticisation of self-infliction, this neatly articulates the fetish's indexing of pain rather than reassurance. But it is crucial to note that this orientation is distinctly spectatorial: in other words, I am not arguing simply for the instatement of masochism in the text but in the audience's approach to the text, an approach that is directed by the film but also exists outside of it. Let us revisit the protagonists' first meeting and see how. While Walter stands at a pronounced distance from Phyllis when she is at the top of, then coming down, the stairs, the shots of her create a pronounced proximity for the spectator, as medium close-ups. In other words, on each occasion there is a gross break from our sharing of Walter's position, from the eye-line matches that frequent the film: we get conspicuously close to Phyllis – speeding tickets do not curtail our movements – in a way that Walter does not or cannot yet. This 'yet' is important here: integral to the masochistic orientation of spectatorship is the issue of the spectator's foreknowledge. The spectators' fetishistic appreciation precedes or rather anticipates Walter's, as does their alignment with masochistic pleasure. Walter will later note his wish to see Phyllis without the 'damned staircase between them', but for us the staircase operates immediately as tease and never as barrier. Her descending the stairs while Walter waits in the drawing room is captured as a close-up on her legs passing behind the metal railings, her anklet appearing and disappearing. This frustrated view – acknowledged by Walter but anticipated by the camera – counters the common cinematic over-emphasis, and certainly un-obscured framing, of the female spectacle. It is typical, instead, of the pleasurable impediments of the masochistic position.

> Masochism obsessively recreates the movement between conceal-ment and revelation, disappearance and appearance, seduction and rejection, in emulation of the ambivalent response to the mother who may either abandon or overwhelm the child. (Studlar 1988: 21–2)

Walter's next visit to Phyllis starts with the repetition of the image of her legs coming down the stairs while he is at an even more pronounced distance, this time actually absent, outside the front door. This sets in motion the repetition-motif of the masochistic text, and one that is to be, again deliberately, owned by the spectator, but it also reiterates the antici-patory mode of masochistic spectatorship, as being ahead of, pre-empting, the protagonists' desires. While the narrative is highly subjective – narrating one man's intense experience, told in extended flashback complete with reflective voice-over – it is not restricted though it might feel like it is. Instead, the heightened subjectivity of the narration is for the spectator specifically. Like the enactment of memories in *The Killers* and *Out of the Past* (and the letter in *Letter from an Unknown Woman*) these masochistic texts are staged and unfold, often self-consciously, as visual spectacle for the spec-tators looking on. In *Double Indemnity* the spectators' gaze, and privileged knowledge through that gaze, is marked as operating independent of and pre-empting Walter's, all in a narrative suffused with the suspenseful, and sensually vibrant, emphasis upon the inevitable and the inescapable. As such, *Double Indemnity* is a quintessentially suspenseful text. Of course, suspense is commonly associated with the thriller, with its tense but gradual piecing together of events. But, often overlooked is the grounding of suspense in predictability, in the heightening of tension through the waiting for something expected and not unknown. In other words, what is often overlooked is its emphatic correspondence to masochism. Suspense, then, further normalises or popularises masochism; it gives masochism a (narrative) method. It also reveals much about the machinations of specta-torship, for where masochism can be attributed to the experience of both characters and spectators, suspense is spectatorial.

Masochism and suspense

> If the creation of curiosity demands that information be withheld from the spectator, the creation of suspense demands that enough information be revealed to the spectator so he or she can anticipate what might happen. (Derry 1988: 31)

The highly-charged wait for anticipated events is the suspenseful thrill fuel-ling the *noir* narrative for its spectators. Such narratives depend upon foreknowledge, upon establishing the knowingness of the participants both within and without the text. This knowingness is created through various routes: the aesthetic or textual (for example, structure, characterisation and visual motif), the spectatorial (for example, shot selection and restricted narration) and the industrial (for example, genre expectations and commercial pre-sell). These routes converge on the site of spectatorship: the spectator's perspective might be privileged in the film's focus upon a repeated gesture as further clue in the formulaic pattern of the suspense narrative which is anticipated by the spectator (whose perspective might be privileged in the focus, for example). Or, to put it more clearly, we are cued before and during the film to notice and suspect certain outcomes from the introduction of iconographic elements: when Kathy, for example, steps out of the shadows in *Out of the Past*, ethereally beautiful but familiarly foreboding, we realise what role she has played in Jeff's past, in the genre's present and in the story's future.

In terms of narrative content and allusion, this knowingness operates also as the repeated referencing of the inevitable or the inescapable or of fate. Inevitability pervades these films most obviously in the typical or formative *noir*s and their narratives that start with the 'end' of the male protagonist. *The Killers* begins with the Swede having been tracked down to his new life by assassins (which echoes in Jeff's discovery at the start of *Out of the Past*). *Double Indemnity* starts with a badly-injured Walter taking up the dictaphone. Nowhere is the 'terminal start' more obvious than in *D.O.A.* whose opening credit sequence charts an endless, rhythmic walk (not that dissimilar from Walter's) down the corridors of a police station, where the now-revealed male protagonist announces to detectives that he has been murdered through a delayed-reaction poison. The narratives that follow such starting positions lead back to the men's always-already demise. Foreknowledge is structured into the films, then, through the privileging of the spectator's gaze, as discussed through *Double Indemnity*, and through a particular narrative pattern. It also operates within the cycle of inevitable emotions that attends masochistic oscillation, that movement between, say, comfort and coldness. Masochistic repetition – of disappointment and dejection, of passionate embraces, of hopeless devotion – suffuses *Out of the Past* in which Jeff's stolid presence folds to Kathy's whims at every turn. He is resolute, he says, each time, and each time he submits. In-between these inevitable submissions then, his protest – that he is over her, knows she is bad – is readily readable as the disavowal of knowledge or activity so integral to both suspense and masochism. The films are full of other kinds of fore-shadowings and returns too. In *Out of the Past* and *The Killers* the women are prefigured as stunning but malignant, as spectres for the spell-bound men. As in *Double Indemnity*, characters appear and reappear. Like the return of the repressed, characters evade neither their past nor their fate, nor the fruition of their unconscious desires.

Such tragic inevitability, and its masochistic core, also plays out in these films through their characters' references to fate, to their unavoidable destinies. This is a familiar tactic of disavowing activity ('it is fate and not my own desire that finds me so cruelly treated') but also of evading responsibility: 'I can't help myself' says Lisa in *Letter from an Unknown Woman* before leaving her husband for Stefan. As Gaylyn Studlar pointed out, following Reik's work, the masochist typically 'displaces responsibility onto fate … [and] masochistic desire masquerades its perverse quest behind the romantic guise of mythical or fateful inevitability' (1994: 50). This side issue, here, of responsibility or rather of the relationship between the spectator's pleasure in submission to the text and its *social implications* will provide the focus of chapter four, where we will address films that are, for want of a better phrase, distinctly dodgy in the kinds of pleasures they afford and the kinds of response that they require. Such films, I will suggest, complicate the 'perversity' of the pleasure that underpins spectatorship. Meanwhile, the contemporary erotic thriller usefully sets up this dynamic between masochistic or 'perverse' pleasures and social context.

The anticipation underwriting both suspense and masochism, then, is a key component of spectatorship. Entering into the realm of fiction and fantasy with anticipation or foreknowledge is, I want to argue, a precondition of narrative cinema. It is a precondition that would strengthen exponentially with the development of the Hollywood film industry, and, especially through its commercial emphasis upon creating and then catering to audience expectation (via genre, stars, the cult of the director, hype, pre-sell and so on). As we turn now to the contemporary erotic thriller, the knowingness of spectatorship becomes increasingly important as the genre reworks its classical roots and proliferates within the technological explosions of the 1980s and 1990s.

Back to Basics

> 'Don't believe what you see, believe what you feel'
> — Violet in *Bound* (1996)

If classic *noir* is indeed intoxicating, the contemporary version, or rather the 1990s surge in its production, is downright drunk and disorderly. Picture *Basic Instinct*'s Detective Nick Curran (Michael Douglas) whose fall from the wagon is framed by public outbursts and dangerous sex. Erotic thrillers like this, *Body of Evidence* and *Bound* are consistent with their forebears in their thematic, aesthetic and, as I will continue to stress, erotic emphases upon masochistic pleasure, but they are far more blatant. One of the questions for the rest of this chapter is what does this on-screen blatancy, this avowal of masochism, lend to our evolving understanding of contemporary spectatorship? The 'dupes' pronounce their self-destructiveness or are told it by their side-kicks or shrinks. The women revel in their sexual sway. Gasps escape, skin is broken, wrists are bound. The films provide soft-core not sobriety, over- rather than under-statement, and in so doing mark out the spectator as demanding of, and unavoidably complicitous in, the erotic pleasure of dangerous if not deadly prospects. In this way these films distil the arousal-potential of popular cinema into a standardised genre format (and one that would find huge success in the emerging home video market). The films, then, both confirm the latent (masochistic) erotics of classical spectatorship and speak specifically to the socio-historical context of 1990s film culture. It is the latter which will matter most here: what the erotic thriller genre tells us about the sexual politics of its Anglo-American context and the, not unconnected, seismic shift in the nature of spectatorship that began during the same period. It is, then, a conjunctural or synthetic analysis of spectatorship that busies us now as we combine issues of social context, textual practice and psychic process to explore how the erotic thriller updates *noir* precisely by recoding its masochistic economy to speak to a different cultural climate. Let us begin by tracing the various ways that the erotic thriller inscribes and incites, or, rather, renders explicit, masochistic pleasure, in order that we may tackle what this explicitness, not simply of sex but of 'perversity', says about those looking on and where they are looking on from.[3]

The three films, *Basic Instinct*, *Body of Evidence* and *Bound*, though I will refer to a larger group, are striking examples of such 1990s fare for specific reasons. *Basic Instinct* represents the milestone film in terms of its financial success, tremendous popularity and critical attention.[3] It triggered the emergence of the erotic thriller as a generic and commercial category (and one that would be retroactively applied).[4] The genre could be thought of as proceeding down two routes, with *Body of Evidence* and *Bound* as representatives of each. In one direction, the soft-core stakes were upped, the formulaic elements intensified and the straight-to-video market for the genre guaranteed. *Body of Evidence*, better than most, represents this excessive genre-adoption/condensation. A self-conscious overdetermination of *noir*ist affect suffuses the film which opens with the camera's chiaroscurist passage through a garden to a bedroom during a stormy night. Sudden lightning flashes serve not just to supplement the atmosphere but perform a blatant sensationalism to the point of possible parody. The second route mapped the expansion and necessary diversification of the genre within Hollywood. This route is perfectly represented by *Bound* in its hybridisation of the gangster, *noir* and romance films, and its convergence of target groups: the straight male and lesbian audience.

These 1990s films' sexual dynamics, and the masochistic economy underwriting them, are no longer limited to the sensual, the structural or subtextual, to heated looks, aggressive kisses and self-defeating acts. Instead, the desire for danger or downfall and the pleasures implicit in painful events, whether literal, imagined or anticipated, are writ large. This large writing appears in several fonts. Firstly, it operates through the presence of sadomasochism: the sexual practice of submission and aggression by either partner in an encounter which, as illustrated above, emerges from the masochistic economy. It is not just that we see more sex in *Basic Instinct* and the films that followed it, but that we see a certain kind of sex. By embellishing the power play of the central pair with the performances and activities, if not the accoutrement, associated with sadomasochism, the erotic thriller popularises and accentuates *noir*'s masochistic legacy as a contemporary event. In the prime example, *Basic Instinct*, Catherine (Sharon Stone) binds the wrists of Nick to the bed posts, drags her nails down his back, taunts him and takes him and then lets him go. The accessories and scenarios of S&M are often employed too. Nowhere is this more overblown, of course, than in *Body of Evidence* where the opening crime yields nipple clamps, and one sexual encounter between Rebecca and Frank involves, among other things, the dripping of wax.

Walter's voice-over comment in *Double Indemnity* about Phyllis's anklet cutting into her leg, as confessed but certainly suppressed declaration of masochistic fascination, is supersized in these contemporary thrillers. So when Rebecca in *Body of Evidence*, flirting with Frank over dinner during their first *tête-à-tête*, comes out as a woman who likes it rough, she does so by telling Frank a typical tale of masochistic origination. The mythologising (or fetishising) of pain, real or imagined, that determines Walter's, and the frame's, investment in Phyllis's anklet, becomes Rebecca's childhood story of how the taste of the strawberries she had picked was so much enhanced by the scraping of her legs in retrieving them. Frank looks on a little too tantalised and then to confirm the story's initiating rite, asks Rebecca to (use her 'SM-play-dar' to) expose a like-minded individual in the restaurant. Looking straight at him, she declares that she will not because 'he doesn't know it yet'. In *Bound* the seduction of Corky (Gina Gershon) by Violet (Jennifer Tilly) starts off with her proclaiming how painful a tattoo on her breast was to have done and, while caressing it with her own fingers and taking Corky's hand to join in, she adds that she loves the way it feels. Part primal scene, part *ur* text, such originating tales function as an obvious come on for the on-screen admirer and, of course, for the spectator. More than this, in *Body of Evidence* especially, it interpellates those looking on as similarly sexually susceptible. Crucially, these come-ons are neither channelled through nor owned solely by the male imaginary – as they are mostly in *noir* – but appear authored by the women and, as such, the films allude to significant changes in sexual politics.[5] I am not suggesting that these films are straightforwardly feminist or progressive – indeed their phobic traditionalisms have been well noted (see Aaron 1994 and 1998; Deleyto 1997; Wallace 2000) – but that the potential for gender fluidity rather than absolutism attends both the on-screen erotic power dynamics and the male and female spectator's response to it. In this way the genre enables what theorists in the last chapter referred to as the mobility of spectatorial positions alongside insisting upon the impact of socio-sexual conditioning.

The films' sexual invitations also often operate independently of the couple's encounters. *Bound* is the best example of this in that its status as sexual cinema (as conferring *to-be-turned-on-ness*) and its sadomasochistic aesthetic (in referencing the sexually sub-cultural) exist beyond the text. It is heavily indebted to *noir*, contains plenty of erotic encounters between the two female protagonists, but no S&M acts take place. Nevertheless, its appeal to sadomasochism is immediate. The film opens not with the defeated male hero, but with Corky bound and gagged on the floor of a closet: rope securing her hands and her feet and a white scarf around her mouth. It is not her inevitable demise that is referenced by this scene nor *noir*'s catalogue of doomed figures who preceded her, but the erotic aesthetic of subjugation, of sexual (mis)adventure. Foetally enfolded in this tight space, there is little doubt that the woman's voice-over – 'I had this image of you, inside of me, like a part of me' – refers to the female character before us. It is through the highly stylised sexualisation of the image that the film will continue, from the camera's heady but oblique descent down the closet, picking out a woman's hat boxes, clothes and stilettos, to the far trashier overtones of soft-core pornography. While the Corky/Violet encounters are absolutely intended to be sexually exciting – it is not just for between-the-sheets cred that the directors employed a sex-consultant to work on the film – the soft-core insinuations operate beyond the couple.[6] Within the first thirteen minutes of the film we have had at least six references to plugging, plumbing and screwing various wet or dripping orifices (beyond, but of course building to and from, Corky actually penetrating Violet). Although licensed, liberally, by Corky's line of work as painter and plumber – clearing out the bath in the apartment she is doing up, rescuing Violet's earring from the kitchen sink's U bend – there is little excuse for the lesbian bar Corky visits being called The Watering Hole. Then again, despite the directors' reputation and the film's new queer credentials, this is, like *Body of Evidence*, a De Laurentiis Production.[7]

The second way in which the erotic thriller renders the masochistic economy of *noir* that much more explicit is through making its object of desire a prime suspect for murder. The 'women' are not prospectively but literally deadly. In *Basic Instinct* and *Body of Evidence* as with a whole host of other examples, like *Jagged Edge* (1985), *Sea of Love* (1989), *A Kiss Before Dying* (1991), *Whispers in the Dark* (1992) and *Sliver* (1993), the 'seduced' figure knows for much if not all of the relationship that the lover might be a murderer. Suspicion of their *a priori* murderousness is not a retroactive problem or irrelevancy, as it was in *Double Indemnity* or *Out of the Past*, but underpins the infatuation. The dupe's/spectator's oscillation between believing the innocence or guilt of the prime suspect/object of desire creates that highly masochistic, and suspenseful, movement between comfort and fear. There are two other recurrent and related themes within these films that further intensify their masochistic charge. The erotic intent (and contemporary investment) of the masochistic dynamic between the central couple is especially pronounced within the emergence of the 'filmic female sexual killer' whose murder of men runs concurrent with orgasm (Aaron 1998). In *Basic Instinct* and *Body of Evidence*, as well as *Sea of Love* and straight-to-video fare *Indecent Behaviour* (1994), sex and danger are merged to the extent that they occur at the same time. A further theme within some erotic thrillers – especially those in which the standard couple is reversed, so that there is a *homme fatal* and a female dupe – is female over-identification. In *Sliver* and *A Kiss before Dying* (as well as the straight-to-video film *Sensation* (1995) not only does the susceptible female fall for the potentially murderous man, but the narratives hinge upon her strong primarily physical connection to a dead woman. This connection is over-determined, and the heroine also occupies, or obsessively comes to occupy, other aspects of the dead woman's identity such as location, lifestyle or relationship. While this maps the woman's 'perverse' desires onto her passage to a correct femininity, so that all of these films end in typical Oedipal fashion with the woman's rejection of the (m)other woman, it adds a powerful aesthetic charge of masochistic inevitability to the narratives for the spectator.

As with Hitchcock's *Rebecca*, in *A Kiss before Dying*, *Sensation* and *Sliver* the heroine over-identifies not just with a dead woman but with a dead woman who was the victim, potentially, of her present lover. Over-identification, in this way, symbolises the heroine's active flirtation with the possibility of death, a sexual self-endangerment. The degree to which the heroine *chooses* this 'perverse' emulation or desire for death, or is aware of their lover's culpability, varies. Rather than just re-laying the tracks of female destiny, then, these texts languish in their heroine's masochism as a prime source of suspense. At the same time, each cinematic act of over-identification builds suspense, charging the narrative with her inevitable demise. This inevitability, this masochistic charge to her over-identification, is accentuated in *A Kiss Before Dying* by Sean Young playing both sisters (Dory who is murdered and Ellen who over-identifies with her). That this was not true of the original film (1955), in which the sisters were played by different actresses, emphasises the intent in the later film, and the shift in emphasis that it suggests. Where Linda Ruth Williams, like Charles Derry, locates this theme of doubling as a sub-category of the genre, Lynda Hart sees it as referencing a demonic femininity and/or lesbianism most aptly evidenced in *Basic Instinct* (Derry 1988; Hart 1994: 124–34; Williams 2005: 35). For me, in enhancing the inevitability integral to the on-screen masochism, it references the knowingness of spectatorship. In addition, rather than representing female entrapment, over-identification here, alongside the films' heavy stylisation of generic elements, allows an exploitation of the female masquerade. These self-consciously skilled performances of the excesses of femininity do not just gesture towards the potential production of 'a problematic within which the image is manipulable, producible, and readable by the woman' (Doane 1999: 143) but achieve it. What is more they make it – and the 'intra-feminine fascinations' (Stacey 1992: 253) underlying female spectatorship – more than available to women, they make them pleasurable.

The contemporary erotic thriller in conferring *to-be-turned-on-ness* provides a telling enactment of the activity inherent in looking on. The genre exposes both the active pleasure of masochism (underlying the on-screen S&M) and the agency inherent in submission (underlying spectatorship itself). But in associating *turned-on-ness* with perversity, such films connect spectators' erotic economy to socially problematic behaviours: not voyeurism but violent sex, fetishes, queerness. The implications of this association need to be set within the 1990s social context, but they must also be thought about in terms of gender. While 'perversity', like turned-on-ness, is accessible to both male and female characters, and spectators, it cannot be divorced from gender considerations. Female masochism brings with it a different set of baggage to male masochism, in terms of the patriarchal association of femininity with masochism, and women's troubled relationship to male violence. Although masochism as a sexual preference has been reclaimed as an active desire, and 'few would now assert that women are "more" masochistic than men' (Fitzpatrick Hanly 1995: 406), female masochism cannot, and to some extent must not, escape its misogynistic background. At the same time, readings of erotic thrillers (of film in general) should maintain a healthy scepticism with regard to the eroticisation of male violence.[8] As Linda Williams points out, 'the recovery of masochism as a form of pleasure does not bode well for a feminist perspective whose political point of departure is the relative powerlessness of women' (1989: 205). Similarly, 'perversity' with the ever-present scare quotes has remained cordoned off as a problem term with a difficult past. Tantalisingly illicit, it must be held at a distance, and there criticised, so that it can be appreciated properly. It is to the tension between the perverse pleasures of spectatorship and their social consequences that we now turn.

Sexual adventurism and social context

Sadomasochism accentuates the traditional roles of the two *noir* protagonists: the dangerousness of the woman, as unconventionally active and aggressive, and the masochism of the man, as submissive and wanting. But of course it does more than this: it locates the erotic thriller amidst cultural trends of 1990s Western culture. In the most general terms, mainstream 1990s cultural products were replete with danger-tinged images and risk-laden narratives, whether it was the latest action or teen-horror film, (another) renaissance of disaster movies, or the leather-clad ads for tyres, sunglasses or perfume.[9] Of course, the dangers and risks that the period favoured were decidedly erotic (Aaron 1999). Outside of the mainstream, the decreasingly marginal practices of sadomasochism and body modification – especially tattooing and piercing – grew in popularity.[10] Indeed, S&M seemed to be 'suddenly everywhere' according to a *New York Magazine* article in 1994 (Blau 1994: 38). This sentiment is expressed by Lynda Hart too in discussing the proliferation of representations of sadomasochism, which she sees as diluting its critical or oppositional value by making S&M sexuality *'nothing in itself* because it is everywhere and everything' (1998: 34). Indeed Lynn Chancer, in her book *Sadomasochism in Everyday Life* (1992), identified masochism within the sexual relationships of the majority.[11]

In the last few decades public awareness or tolerance of sadomasochistic role-play and sexual exploration has been reflected within culture, within criticism and within private relationships. It is not surprising then that the period would also see a burgeoning interest in film noir as an area of critical inquiry, or the production of neo-*noir* films.[12] The reclaiming of masochism as an active, even a positive, desire by psychoanalysts and cultural theorists post-Freud, occurred most vociferously in the 1990s. Numerous studies came out during this period after Deleuze's incisive reclaiming of Sacher-Masoch's work in *Masochism: Coldness and Cruelty* in 1991.[13] The 1990s popular indulgences in male masochism – which *Basic Instinct* and *Body of Evidence* certainly contribute to – dovetailed with the concept's radical aspirations, reflecting its 'theoretical renaissance in which the erotics of submission have been reclaimed by a diverse group of scholars as an emancipatory sexuality for men' (Hart 1998: 87). Certainly Michael Douglas's star persona sits firmly within the decade's distinction of the 'new man' or the 'metrosexual' (Simpson 1994a and 1994b: 22; Savran 1998: 206–10). He is vulnerable, even victimised, and potentially going down for (and on) his female lover. Identified as a key player in the emerging genre by Linda Ruth Williams in his 'wounded survivor role', she finds him 'acutely symptomatic of the masculinities of his moment' (2005: 194), albeit without reference to masochism.

The decade's sexual curiosity also showed up as sadomasochism in mainstream comedies, such as *Exit to Eden* (1994) and *Preaching to the Perverted* (1997), which grounded their humour in the seeming bizarreness of fetishism and the contrast between the respectable, average individual and the den of iniquity in which they find themselves. In both films, S&M is a source of comedy but also meant to be somewhat appealing. It is appealing in terms of its status as fun, rather than it being contagious in terms of its status as sickness. This latter status determined the long-standing imaging of sexual deviants within Hollywood's repertoire of psychopaths as epitomised by William Freidkin's *Cruising* (1980), cinema's most notorious depiction of sadomasochism. The comedies testify to S&M's erotic encoding and integration into the popular imagination but the depictions are tame. The stylised sadomasochism in these films (as in the non-mainstream Sex Film[14]) becomes an almost requisite element of titillation or shorthand sign for sexual freedom.

At the eye of the AIDS crisis, the equation of sex and danger or sex and death is hardly surprising, and several theorists have asserted their co-mingling within popular culture, and especially within cinema both in terms of the metaphors for AIDS operating in the mainstream, and as the emergence of the New Queer Cinema, with which *Bound* can be associated (see Arroyo 1993; Pearl 1999 and 2004). The erotic thrillers sit amidst other cultural anxieties – those attending postmodernism and its dissolution of subjectivity, or pre-millenial angst – but other fascinations too. The 1990s, and its creation of the filmic female sexual killer, must be situated within the real-time attention to female sexual murderers. The decade provided the first, Aileen Wuornos, arrested in 1991, and then the second, Rosemary West, arrested in 1994. The figure's transcription onto the big screen in the form of Catherine Trammel sits amidst this bigger picture, and the ever growing cultural interest in what Jane Caputi (1988) earlier categorised as an age of sex crime.

The final crucial context for understanding the erotic thriller genre, and especially its exposure of the sexualisation of spectatorship, is an industrial one. The period of its evolution held two major advances in infotainment technology. The first, in 1991, was the birth of the World Wide Web whose sexual potential 'was manifest from the start' (Williams 2005: 7). The second was the invention of the VCR and the resulting explosion in home viewing which meant 'you could watch whatever you wanted, whenever you wanted with whoever you wanted, in privacy' (ibid.). The erotic thriller genre, as Linda Ruth Williams argues, was integral to the expansion of this home market. These technological advances had an enormous impact on the power, and especially the erotic power, of looking on. Firstly, they represented a seismic shift in the nature of spectatorship: the cinema ceased to be the only or, later, the main site for watching films.[15] Secondly, the relocation of spectatorship to the home (or the 'personal' computer) represented a privatisation of the perverse pleasures afforded by film. This new *sofa spectatorship* clearly has serious implications for our understanding of the (hypothetical) agency of the spectator, and for the illicit fantasies sanctioned, if not summoned, by the darkened auditorium. The spectator could now control the image (via the rental market, and the remote control), and own the image (via the retail market). If, as Mulvey indicated, the frozen narrative was the erotically contemplated one, and deferral and repetition characterise masochistic fantasy, then it is little wonder that with its pause, slow motion and repeat capabilities the VCR and the erotic thriller were instantly compatible.

In their sexual self-consciousness the films under discussion mean to arouse the audience through their use of distinctly adult material. Asked whether this was a clear aim of his, director Paul Verhoeven happily admits: 'Not for the whole of *Basic Instinct* … but certainly for the two big scenes' (quoted in Williams 2004: 19). In addition to the erotic interactions of characters in the films, the developing genre of the erotic thriller tells another story about the sexual mores and social interests of the period.

It immediately speaks to a relatively relaxed period in Hollywood history, when the sexual cinema of Verhoeven, among others, was embraced by the mainstream. This is always partly retroactive; the relative permissiveness of the Clinton era has been rendered that much more striking after the fact, most notably with the conservatism of Bush Junior's presidency. As Linda Ruth Williams put it, in accounting for why 'Hollywood doesn't do sex like it used to ... One answer is George W. Bush' (2004: 18).

The seemingly sexually relaxed period of the 'naughty nineties' was also associated with various sex scandals on both sides of the Atlantic. From the 'Tailhook '91' controversy (when 83 women and seven men were sexually assaulted during the 35th annual air force convention in Las Vegas), to the various charges brought against Bill Clinton himself, climaxing (no, really) in his impeachment by the House of Representatives in 1998. In Britain, Conservative Prime Minister John Major's moral impera-tives in his 'back to basics' campaign backfired as two of his ministers were exposed as having extramarital affairs (David Mellor in 1992, Tim Yeo in 1993). Even more significant was the sensational auto-erotic death of MP for Eastleigh, Stephen Milligan, who was found suspender-ed on his kitchen table in February 1994. Increased attention to such sexual (mis)practices followed in the media. For example, the *Guardian* reported the growing concern at the number of children engaging in 'pleasurable asphyxiation' and the participation of an 'aiding' party (Anon. 1995b: 12), and the *New York Times* reported on cases of sexual strangulation (Anon. 1994: B4). Then of course there was pop star Michael Hutchence's assumed auto-erotic death in 1997.[16]

The public sphere appeared open to information about sexual behav-iours: certainly the entering into public discourse of auto-erotic asphyxia-tion represented a huge advance in educating people about a previously silenced cause of death.[17] However, the tolerance or liberalism that this might imply cannot go unchecked, for this period also witnessed significant attempts to curb sexual liberties. In other words, as individual 'perversity' threatened to be absorbed into cultural diversity via popular culture, the boundaries between 'them' and 'us' needed to be firmly reinforced. Such reinforcement was certainly occurring within the judiciary. In Europe this was epitomised by the Brown case, or Operation Spanner as the well-publi-cised three-year-long police investigation in Britain was called. Sixteen gay men who were arrested and sentenced for consensual S&M activities in 1987 would appeal the case over the following decade. The European Commission's reconsideration in March 1997 upheld the British government's right to prosecute the men, and its definition of perversity which hinged on the impossibility of masochistic agency. Despite the 'victims' asking for the pain that was inflicted, the State was deemed correct to judge their request a symptom of sickness rather than subjectivity. In the United States, Clinton's attempts to overturn the ban on gay military personnel in 1993 met with stark opposition and considerable amendment. Indeed, the number of discharges on the grounds of homosexuality increased under his 'Don't ask, Don't tell, Don't pursue' policy, and 'harassment of gay and lesbian personnel appears to have intensified'.[18] While the decade saw the first push for same-sex marriage – in Hawaii in 1993 – its most formidable outcome was the Defence of Marriage Act, which naturalised heterosexuality within the Constitution itself and hence within Federal law. Signed by Clinton upon re-election in 1996, such acts would proliferate at state level.

What I want to suggest by this discussion is not the strict opposition of sexual liberties and sexual constraints, as a kind of lash and backlash of permissiveness, nor to promote a wishy-washy to-ing and fro-ing of cultural practices as the necessary pattern of social change. Instead, I am arguing that the cultural indulgence in perverse pleasures taking place, for example, through film, is *managed* by the social definitions of perversity, both legislative and otherwise, taking place elsewhere. By these other social definitions I mean the public's distancing reactions to representations of oppositional behaviours or perversity that occur in the pages of tabloids (especially in the reporting of, say, the Brown case), in the lobby of cinemas as audiences flood out (of *Basic Instinct* for example), and invisible but rife in the everyday, what Anita Phillips has called the 'disgust' that greets masochism: the tut-tuts, shielded smiles and feigned surprise at the latest shocking details (1998: 75).

If 'perverse' pleasure is outed (and normalised) and masochism is avowed on-screen and in other cultural productions, the disavowal of activity and responsibility integral to the distinction and enjoyment of masochism must shift to someplace else.[19] Indeed, it is precisely a sense of agency – of implication, of complicity – that the distancing reactions work to resist. Of course, this is only a *faux* resistance – the smile shielded, the shock feigned – and, as in the masochistic contract, the disavowal of agency is pleasure's essential ingredient. In other words there is a delicate balance between the perverse pleasures of spectatorship and their acknowledgement, which is a key reason why audience studies are so partial: the spectator's response after the fact is not always, indeed is rarely, in league with the spectator's experience. This is not to say that you cannot believe what people say but that their comments must, as Ien Ang suggested (1985: 11), be read as texts themselves, and that audience studies must incorporate an understanding of the social and psychic complexities of spectatorship. Hence, those engaged in reception research often target the lesser-censored self-pronouncements on film found in chat rooms or news groups on the internet, or encouraged by well-placed invitations in specific magazines asking people to share their intimate reactions to cinema by private correspondence. A fine example of this is Thomas Austin's (1999) study of the reception of *Basic Instinct* amongst straight men and adolescent males. Not only did it confirm the sexualisation of spectatorship exploited by the film, and the illicitness that it depends upon, but Austin provided useful insight into the triangulation of text, psyche and context. He illustrated how the negotiation of the film's meaning took place through textual provocation and industrial pre-sell, but also through the *interpersonal* realm. The significance of social context to spectatorship must be expanded, therefore, to include an understanding of how peer pressure and moral imperatives shaped the young men's readings: Austin notes, for example, the 'kudos', 'social disapproval' and 'embarrassment of watching sex scenes in public' (1999: 158). Integral to their negotiated responses then was their indulgence in certain elements of the film (Stone's sexiness) and their distancing from others (the 'bad sex', where Nick 'rapes' his ex-girlfriend). According to Austin, 'the violence inherent in Nick's sexuality is negotiated ... through attempts to divorce it from the heterosexual desire that the spectator shares with the character, and to expel it as "sickening" and "obscene"' (ibid.). For me, this attempted expulsion of the socially problematic recognises spectatorship for what it is: a negotiation (articulated, as ever, through disavowal) between one's involuntary participation, one's *turned-on-ness*, and the agency inherent in submission to cinema's perverse pleasures and the ethical framework that such a negotiation requires. What is so interesting about the categorisation of the 'obscene' is precisely its capacity to bridge all these. As Wayne Booth put it, in his work on ethics and reading:

How do you decide that a story is obscenely pornographic? ... You can do so only by 'listening' to it, discovering what your mind and body do in response, and confessing to the world that you have found something obscene in it – that is, made something obscene out of it. Only in intimacy with obscenity can one know what is obscene. (1988: 140)

It is to our intimacy with 'obscenity', our complicity in the representation of the socially unacceptable, to an ethics of spectatorship that we now turn.

4   ETHICS AND SPECTATORSHIP: RESPONSE, RESPONSIBILITY AND THE MOVING IMAGE

People love to look. I am not just referring to the lurid pleasures of witnessing something illicit or gruesome, but to the banality of everyday media that revolves, frequently, around the individual's inclination to sit back and visually consume information or entertainment. Where classical cinema is built upon the age-old popularity of public performance – from coliseum, to carnival, to cabaret – television took this ever-dominating leisure practice to the latest outlet.

Film, like all visual culture, provides us with the possibility, and the pleasure, of seeing things we would not normally be able to see: a stranger turning on her home computer, feeding the cat, flossing her teeth; a soldier wounded in battle; a car chase; two people, or more, making love. So far so obvious: cinema makes a spectacle of the everyday and turns the spectacular into commonplace content. But what does it actually mean that spectatorship revolves around our sharing in or witnessing the private or intimate acts of others, or that it depends upon our enjoyment of events that often represent a gross break with legal or social mores? That film frequently scorns the boundaries that govern real life, be they mortal or moral, is, of course, part of its charm, and readily licensed through it being a fictional form as well as its ready punishment of corrupt or cruel characters. So on one hand the irreverent or irregular behaviours that films depict, and in certain ways promote, are harmless because they are not real, not true, and certainly not in any way representative (or rather not representative of anything other than film characters). On the other, such behaviours are harmless because they are either categorised or castigated in the film itself as in some way wrongful.

Despite such safeguards, however, the subject of spectatorship has remained framed by furious debate about the damage that art can do, and the practice of it within the public sphere has been regulated through various bodies restricting content, exhibition or admission. The interest in the repercussions of representation is an ancient one, with censorship talk tracking all the way from Plato through to McCarthy or Mary Whitehouse. The will to socially control culture is underwritten by notions of legal or political paternalism that rest on the principle that the state must intervene to protect its guileless, and certainly powerless, subjects from cultural products' ill-effects. This thorny subject, which wagers social control and damage limitation against freedom of speech and individual agency, lies at the heart of the media effects debate, its most popular contemporary forum. In reiterating the critical play-off between the passive spectator and active agent such debates reiterate the existing preoccupations of this book but this time locate them in a distinctly socio-political context. Most importantly, such debates render spectatorship as not simply a speculative or default site for ideological endorsement or multicultural multiplicity, but as a live venue for testing out the limits and resonance of public and private, good and bad taste, conformity and subversion, social agency and moral implication. In other words, it becomes easy to see how spectatorship is ethically loaded, that is, that it represents a negotiation of personal pleasures and others' interests. While I am little concerned here with the damage that film can do the spectator, I believe the service or disservice – and this was a tricky word to decide upon while steering clear of the shackles of moralising – we do ourselves and others via current film culture to be a crucial but markedly under-attended issue of contemporary spectatorship.

This chapter focuses on the ascription of spectatorial agency as a marker of socio-political responsibility. What is meant by this will become clear as the chapter progresses but, for now, let me clarify that spectatorship – which has never happened in a vacuum even if it did for a while occur in a fairly controlled environment – represents an understanding reached between the spectator and culture. This understanding is of growing ethical import. While, as I will argue, ethics has always been relevant to spectatorship, it has become ever more important for several reasons. First, because contemporary or postmodern filmmakers increasingly exploit the contractual nature of spectatorship. Second, because, for various reasons, mainstream films sometimes contain 'unconscionable' content. Third, because those previously mentioned safeguards – films' fiction-status and moral judgements – have diminished both in effect and frequency. Not only do more mainstream films evade moral frameworks or closure – hence the unconscionable content – but the divide between fact and fiction, between the real and the fake 'devastating spectacle' is blurrier, more banal or potentially powerful, than ever. Watching the destruction of downtown New York on a video rental of *Armageddon* (1998) one autumn evening-in, and watching it happen on the same screen the next day 'for real', raises questions not simply about what filmmaking entails, but what looking on does. After all, the production context of each filming was very different, but the spectatorial one – especially as the footage became ever more edited and editorialised, that is narrative-oriented – was strikingly similar.

It is not then a straightforward question of content that preoccupies us now, but a question of consent to it on the part, the participatory part, of the spectator. Edging ever further from the impotence of psychoanalytic theory in the field of social change and from the wishy-washy wide embrace of social theory, our embodied spectator, possibly perverse in her fantasies and diverse in her experience, possesses agency even, if not especially, in her submission. Finally, she must now be held accountable for it.

This chapter falls into two parts. In the first, I will build upon the concept of the contractual alliance between (masochistic) spectator and text, introduced in chapter three, in order to track two cinematic routes to the spectator's complicity. In the second part, I will explore the ethical dimensions attending this dialogue between spectatorship and issues of responsibility, a dialogue that amplifies with the hyper-mediation of violence and the democratisation of technology, both of which redefine and resituate the spectator. What we are left with is the individual continually confronted with images of others' suffering, where recourse to fantasy and other distancing devices becomes either untenable or unethical. The discussion ends then with a move away from the disinterests of theory, or the best interests of politics, to make some unavoidably embodied, and philosophically enriched, conclusions about contemporary spectatorship.

Spectatorial responsibility I: self-reflexivity and the complicitous spectator[1]

Notions of masochism require questions of consent; notions of sadism absent them. This was one of the findings of the last chapter, that the masochist not only wills but seeks 'his' own suffering, and in doing so consents to it, although the disavowal of this consent is integral to 'his' pleasure and the masochistic economy. Sadism cannot characterise spectatorship for it opposes complicity, where spectatorship, like masochism, is by nature contractual. A contractual alliance operates between spectator and text as it does between masochist and 'pseudo-sadist', a relationship founded upon an agreed acting out, or fulfillment, of the masochist's needs, and, hence, its rejection of actual sadism: 'the masochistic contract implies not only the necessity of the victim's consent, but his ability to persuade … to train his torturer' (Deleuze 1991: 75). Gaylyn Studlar's confirmation of the masochistic rather than sadistic motivation of spectatorial pleasures, asserted the consensuality of the masochistic relationship, the 'mutual agreement between partners' (1988: 23), thus equating the contractual alliance of the masochist and his/her partner with the contractual alliance between the spectator and the screen:

> A willing volunteer in cinema's perverse intimacy, the spectator, like the masochist's partner, is not coerced into the alliance … Cinema is not a sadistic institution but preeminently a contractual one based upon the promise of certain pleasures. The masochist requires an audience to make humiliation and pain meaningful. Similarly, the cinematic apparatus is meaningless without a spectator to its exhibitionistic acting out. (1988: 182)

Within the contractual alliance between spectator and film, the dynamic is about masochism and not sadism. If sadism is characterised by the involuntariness of the victim, then neither the masochist nor the spectator, who are by definition consenting, can be imposed upon by the sadism of cinema but rather their masochism directs the narratives. While films, especially those that revel in gratuitous violence, often contain strictly villainous figures who do little else but maim or murder, such a character, though not masochistic him or herself, nevertheless 'is a pure element of masochism' (Deleuze 1991: 42).

So the masochist agrees to – both desires and requires – the other party's infliction of pain within a consensual dynamic. In other words, spectatorship is characterised by complicity even though it depends upon its suppression for its smooth running. This conclusion arises not only from the masochistic model proposed in chapter three but from the classical model too: this is not our first brush with the contractual nature of spectatorship. The classical model was grounded in a similar set-up. Let us revisit it that we may further see how the spectator's fantasy is at stake in his or her consent. In the masochistic model, consent is a disavowed but crucial element in the accomplishment of the fantasy (of victimhood). In what has come to be seen as the sadistic model, consent is the disavowed but crucial element in the accomplishment of the fantasy (of mastery). Both depend upon an exaggeration of fantasy, a disavowal of their reality (which for masochists is that they are doing rather than being done to, and for hypothetical spectators that what they are watching is all an illusion).

At the core of 1970s cine-psychoanalysis, was the concept that film depends upon the spectator accepting an illusion as a form of reality. This acceptance works as a tacit agreement, a kind of contract, between spectator and spectacle. The terms of this contract run something like this: 'I'll forget that you're fake, as long as you help.' In other words, the spectator suspends her disbelief, she 'forgets' she is watching a contrived fabrication, a film, as long as she is encouraged to do so. This is a two-way process; it requires an artful forgetting on both sides of the screen, for the spectator but also for the spectacle itself. As Christian Metz states of the spectacle: 'I watch it, but it doesn't watch me watching it. Nevertheless, it knows that I am watching it' (1982: 94). Thus the relationship between these two, between the spectacle and the spectator, is revealed as an 'active complicity which works both ways' (ibid.).

Now there is much more at stake in this art-full forgetting than just a good night out at the multiplex. Indeed, this process is usefully described by Metz as a 'fundamental disavowal' (ibid.), and needs to be seen as performing an important psychological function for the spectator, an exercise of self-consolidation rooted in fetishism. In chapters one and two we considered the psychological and patriarchal reassurances underlying Freudian fetishism, in which the small child displaces his anxieties about his mother's penis-less state by overvaluing something else. Here, this presents us with a neat paradigm both for understanding the machinations of human behaviour when confronted with something troubling, and, more specifically, for explaining how fetishism connects to the spectacle.

Film, as Kaja Silverman puts it in line with Metz, 'covers over the absent real with a simulated or constructed reality' and in so doing, she adds, 'makes good the spectating subject's lack, restoring him or her to an imaginary wholeness' (1988: 10). In this way, the cinematic spectacle, with all its appeals to authenticity, stands in for reality thereby reassuring the spectator that nothing is amiss. This fetishistic process fortifies the spectator's sense of self and, crucially, depends upon the spectator supporting the cover up. The spectator willingly 'buys' this, this substitution of the spectacle for the real, thereby disavowing the absence of reality, and, as I will come to argue, his or her complicity in the cover up.

What needs to be emphasised is that disavowal is a defensive mechanism. It staves off that which is threatening; it allows one to indulge in fantasy without suffering the consequences of it. The necessary and necessarily safe distance between the spectator and the dangers suggested by and within the cinematic spectacle, be they emotional or psychological (or even ethical), is maintained through disavowal. Disavowal, then, represents a contract between spectator and screen; a contract that sustains the safety of the spectator, licensing a safe indulgence in the unreal, with the promise that it is only temporary: when the spectacle stops, so too will the submission to it as real. The contract says I will engage with you as if this is real, and yet rests upon the fact that it is not to fuel my interest. This paradigm underwrites the film's management of perverse desire (its socio-moral scale) and illusion (its fiction-status).

What I want to do is challenge the spectator's removal and innocence with regard to the spectacle, and argue instead not simply for the spectator's complicity in its creation and endurance, but for the spectator's complicity in its often disturbing content. I turn then to a set of films that make a clear case for this, that are contra-disavowal. They deliberately break that cinematic contract between spectator and screen in two key, and not unrelated, ways: firstly, by aggravating the act of 'artful forgetting' at the heart of the spectacle-real dynamic; secondly, by pushing the limits of what can be accepted by the spectator, indeed, what is acceptable. These two are interrelated in that, as will become obvious, it is the film's self-reflexivity – its anti-forgetting strategy – that renders the material so difficult to take.

Breaking the contract

Peeping Tom (1960), *The Eyes of Laura Mars* (1978) and *Strange Days* (1996) represent a certain trajectory of the heavily self-conscious or self-reflexive mainstream film that has seen its numbers swell in recent years as the tropes of postmodernism proliferate on the big and, with the popularity of reality television, little screen. Basically, self-reflexive narratives draw attention to themselves as texts, as artificial, mediated (re)presentations. They can do this in a variety of ways that impact upon the text's form and content. They might be about visual arts, performance or filmmaking, or contain the machinery of their production. They might point out the devices of the medium or the signifiers of cinema, or of viewing, with recurrent images of cameras or of eyes. They might be about the pleasures of looking, or the fear of it, the lure of voyeurism or the dangers encountered. They might knowingly reference or borrow from other texts. Each of the selected narratives revolves around visual images and their production and use. *Peeping Tom* focuses on film, *The Eyes of Laura Mars* on photography and *Strange Days* on a form of video. The murder plots of each make their relationship to the pleasures and dangers of looking especially fraught.

It is not just that these films are about image-making or image-watching (so many films are) or that they suggest that both are entangled with dangers and delights (so many films do), but that they firmly incorporate the spectator into their narratives while heavily restricting the reassurances on offer. Each film merges the gaze of the image-maker, the image-viewer and the spectator, and does so in the most publicly and personally violent of situations. That it is also the gaze of the murderer, potential victim and spectator that is merged, spectatorial implication becomes loaded with sadomasochistic intent. In *Peeping Tom*, Mark stabs women with the blade attached to the tripod of his camera, the victim watches herself being killed in a mirror attached to the front of the camera. We, the audience, simultaneously, watch the action through the crosshairs of the camera lens. In *The Eyes of Laura Mars*, Laura (Faye Dunaway), via extra-sensory perception (ESP), witnesses the murders of other women, and then at the climax of the film, 'sees' the murderer pursuing her. In the futuristic *Strange Days*, 'playback' technology allows videoed events to be 'enjoyed' as lived experience via special headgear. The playback-spectator's vision fills the screen as subjective narration for the similarly all-seeing film spectator.

Artful reminders

Primarily, these highly self-reflexive films inhibit the spectators' ability to do that 'artful forgetting' by consistently reminding us that we are watching a film. We cannot suppress our status as spectators for the films are all about spectatorship. The radical charge of this, of this spotlighting of the spectator's experience (as the films' self-consciously merged-perspectives make evident) is a fundamental avowal of the real. However, this radical charge is not a given in all self-reflexive films. Indeed, film studies' theorisation of self-reflexivity has found it capable of being either conservative or transgressive (See Feuer 1986; Hedges 1991: 13).

What self-reflexivity's radical function depends upon, and what discussions of it negotiate, is the spectator's distance from the effects of the text. Self-reflexivity is positioned against the self-protecting function of fetishism, of disavowal: it reveals what should be covered up. It would seem, in this way, to be fundamentally interventionist. Yet this situation is easily recouped for more conservative ends. Talking about the musical, Jane Feuer (1986) found the key purpose of its self-reflectivity, as she calls it, to perpetuate the 'myth of spontaneity' and its attendant pleasures of fantasy, through naturalising artificiality itself.[2] This is achieved through masking the artificiality of the spontaneous performance in two main ways: either by concealing the technology that accompanies it or through overwhelming, distracting from, the sense of contrivance with the depiction of characters' innate energy and/or sincerity (see Dyer 1986). So, for example, in *Singin' in the Rain* we have a scene in which Gene Kelly's character sings a love song to Kathy on an unused stage set, and his exuberance outshines the camera lights he manipulates.

In the horror genre, within which we could locate my sample of films, self-reflexivity similarly serves to emphasise the pleasures particular to the genre, in this case, the creation of fear, and does so through implicating the spectator.[3] Carol Clover, questioning the frequency of, and obsession with, imaging eyes in horror film, sees the goal of this form of self-reflexivity as the promotion of fear through audience identification and implication, and sees *Peeping Tom* as a 'horror metafilm: a film that has as its task to expose the psychodynamics of specularity and fear' (1992: 169).

In reminding the spectator that she is watching a film, she is made aware of herself as spectator. This awareness can allay fear, for in exposing its own artificiality, the risk-laden experience is made safe: unreal and distant. Alternatively, self-reflexivity can seem to accentuate the horror by bringing it closer to home, by drawing the spectator in. Self-consciousness in the film breeds self-consciousness in the audience. If terrible things happen to the viewers depicted in the film itself then one's status as viewer seems especially fraught. Both of these positions argue for the spectator's implication but to opposing ends, so what gives a self-reflexive horror film its radical edge? How and why might we distinguish *Peeping Tom*, *The Eyes of Laura Mars* and *Strange Days*?

For Feuer, the musical used self-reflexivity to strengthen rather than undermine the spectacular-ness of the spectacle. The devices of the medium were exposed in order that the devices of the character appeared that much more powerful, honest and natural in their singularity. In *Peeping Tom*, *The Eyes of Laura Mars* and *Strange Days* such qualities are, understandably, absent. However, the visual excesses of the monsters or gore which saturate the horror genre could be seen as a kind of spectacular displacement of the reality check of self-reflexivity, but this visual excess is lacking from these three films. While the three films perpetuate what might be called the 'myth of psychopathology' that the genre requires, the murderers in *Peeping Tom*, *The Eyes of Laura Mars* and *Strange Days* are almost banally evil: denied extraordinariness or singularity. Primarily, they are duplicitous in hiding their identity as murderer. That the identity of the murderer is not revealed in the narrative, and to the spectator, until the final scenes in *The Eyes of Laura Mars* and *Strange Days*, their murderers could be anyone. In merging the view of the murderer with ours they are always 'everyone', always more than themselves. The frame is also often multiple. It is filled with not a point-of-view shot but with what might called a 'points-of-view' shot, one that combines multiple viewpoints, that merges the vision of murderer, victim and spectator.

The Eyes of Laura Mars and *Strange Days* will finally reveal their monsters. The latter subsequently indulges in a range of other classical codes (like romantic union and equilibrated closure) and yet its self-reflexivity is the most shocking. Its points-of-view shots of the most gruesome murder are the most difficult to take. Where *Peeping Tom* has the crosshairs of the lens through which the murderer is filming, and *The Eyes of Laura Mars* a haziness to the image to label the scenes of murder, *Strange Days* offers no such distancing devices. Indeed, it goes all-out to make the superimposition of the shared experience seamless. Perhaps it can afford to with its later compromises to convention, but nevertheless its focus is not just the self-reflexive spectacle but the self-reflexive spectator. While I am suggesting that the former breeds the latter, *Strange Days* makes this explicit. As Laura Rascaroli notes of Bigelow's film, 'the screen, barrier between the auditorium and the action, between fiction and reality, disappears. The spectator's eye is *there*, in the film space' (1998).

Returning to Metz's earlier point about disavowal and the cinematic spectacle, that 'I watch it, but it doesn't watch me watching it', the thing about the spectacle in *Peeping Tom*, *The Eyes of Laura Mars* and *Strange Days* is precisely that it does watch me watching it. In other words, in these films visual images are seen to be created, and created to be seen. Not only is the external spectator incorporated into the highly subjective image, but the internal spectator is utterly aware of herself as spectator as in those horrendous moments of spectatorial realisation: the victim's face in *Peeping Tom*, Laura's despair in *The Eyes of Laura Mars* and Lenny's contortions in *Strange Days*. Nowhere is the excessive presence of the spectator more evident than in *The Eyes of Laura Mars* in which, ostensibly, we receive two Lauras when her vision merges with that of the murderer who is looking at her. In making the spectator her own spectacle, the dismantling of the spectator/spectacle divide is guaranteed.

Not only do the films incorporate the spectator but the spectator's response. In this way we are presented with very clear (moral) guidelines of how to react to these difficult spectacles – except in *Peeping Tom*. Where watching a murder is a source of trauma for Laura in *The Eyes of Laura Mars* and for Lenny in *Strange Days*, for Mark it is a pleasure, and one that he indulges in over and over again, in his repeat murders and in watching and re-watching the films of his murderous acts. The only witness to Mark's murders is his blind landlady who wanders into his home cinema: his room where he is screening his footage. The spectator is noticeably denied an on-screen set of eyes, a surrogate self who gets to be appalled by Mark's acts, and, as such, the film opens itself to charges that it lacks an ethical framework. It is in a similar vein that our being encouraged to feel sympathy for Mark courts controversy. It is little wonder that *Peeping Tom* would cause such a storm.

Acceptance and the acceptable

Michael Powell's *Peeping Tom* stands as a landmark film in terms of the controversy that it generated and, consequently, the directorial career that it compromised. But, as Adam Lowenstein notes, what was so troubling to its critics is not the film's horrors but their insinuation, not what was depicted but how the spectator was so successfully implicated within it. The film drew, he notes, 'resistant viewers into a recognition of their own reflection within this mass culture' (2000: 224).

The implicatedness of the spectator has been a popular theme within the critical reception of all the films under discussion. Lucy Fischer and Marcia Landy saw the primary function of the self-reflexivity of *The Eyes of Laura Mars* as the implication of the spectator within the depiction of violence against women, that is within the (male) sadism of cinema, and 'a world where there is no escape from media manipulation, psychopathology and aggression (1987: 75).

In the inevitability of this violence, self-reflexivity is a coercive force, yet it remains intimately connected to the issue of responsibility – the spectator's complicity in the perpetuation of this violent world. Silverman raises a related issue in her discussion of *Peeping Tom*, a film which also portrays extreme violence towards women whilst emphatically aligning the spectator with the murderer. For Silverman, as for me, *Peeping Tom*'s self-reflexivity exposes the mythic processes at the heart of classical cinema: the safe distances that characterise (fetishistic) spectatorship:

> A recurrent motif in the murder sequences ... functions as a powerful metaphor for the barrier Mark tries to erect between himself and his victims so as to dissociate himself from them, and thereby consolidate his own claim to the paternal legacy. Here, too, Mark's project converges with classic cinema, which also turns upon the fiction that an irreducible distance isolates the viewer from the spectacle. (1988: 34)

It is the navigation of these safe distances by these self-reflexive films that lies at the heart of this discussion.

Self-reflexivity questions the spectator's mythic distance and safety, the irresponsibility or neutrality of looking on. It performs that radical Brechtian practice of distanciation, drawing attention to the myth of separation, of dissociation, and the necessary fiction of self-coherence.[4] But the line between a representation perpetuating or critiquing conventional myths – merely unfolding or instead shattering them – is a thin one, perhaps based upon the rigour or optimism of certain theorists or the quirkiness of certain writers or filmmakers, as the contrary opinions of horror (as misogynist or as parodic) testify. Self-reflexivity appears a major strategy of implication, a deep faultline in the reassurances of spectatorship, and as it becomes all the more frequent and psychodynamically charged, so the viewer's implication becomes that much more apparent.

The self-reflexivity of *Peeping Tom*, *The Eyes of Laura Mars* and *Strange Days* makes the content of the films difficult to take not just because of what they show us, but because of their insistence that we are more than implicated in what they show us. What is more, the films need to be seen as both acknowledging and exploiting the complicity that lies at the heart of spectatorship, that lubricates the spectacle/real dynamic underlying our engagement with cinema. As the spectacle and, for that matter, the real become increasingly socially problematic – with, for example, the unconscionable acts depicted in Michael Haneke's work, for example, or performed on 9/11 – the issue of the spectator's part in these productions becomes ever more pressing.

Spectatorial responsibility II: Dogme, delusion and discomfort

The contractual nature of spectatorship lies, I would suggest, at the heart of the Danish film movement, Dogme 95. For this reason alone it commends itself to our discussion. But its published Manifesto and Vow of Chastity – in which it lists its aims and rules in filmmaking – replete with religious zeal and radical aspirations, seem bent on the realisation of filmmaking's ethical potential and as such Dogme 95 enters the chapter as an essential case study. The Manifesto and Vow (penned by Lars von Trier and co-signed by him and Thomas Vinterberg 'on behalf of Dogme 95'), work as a contract, not only on the part of the filmmakers but always also for the spectators. The Manifesto represents the contractual agreement between the directors associated with the Dogme collective, but this contract impacts on both filmmaking and film-taking. It determines the Dogme product and international recognition of its films and directors, thereby, necessarily, impacting upon the audience in terms of marketing, targeting and tunnel-ling of expectations. But the contract must also be seen as part of the film experience, as representing and informing the relationship between spectator and text. The fervour seasoning the document and the films is not just biblical but contractual. It makes perfect sense then that the vow as a statement of commitment, and a taking of responsibility, should be signed and dated. That the vow fills the screen preceding Dogme films and is incorporated into the watching of them is not just a further display of this commitment, but underlines the contractual nature between the different parties involved. It is about branding for sure, but it is also about audience foreknowledge, expectation and consent.

Like the three examples just discussed, Dogme films are preoccupied with the complicity of those looking on, but it is not self-reflexivity that funds this preoccupation – despite it being a self-reflexive cinema, albeit by default – but some higher quest for truth, as the Vow confirms: 'My supreme goal is to force the truth out of my characters and settings. I swear to do so by all means necessary and at the cost of any good taste and any aesthetic considerations' (von Trier, quoted in Stevenson 2003: 23). A phil-osophically weighty and morally burdened term, truth, for von Trier and the Dogmatics, is, primarily, that which opposes illusion. Illusions represent the cosmeticised, decadent and superficial trickery of mainstream film. Truth, in contrast, resides in the undressed-ness of characters and settings, where sound, action and colour emerge untampered with, to be 'naturally' apprehended within the everyday by the hand-held camera of the Dogme crew. There is more at stake here than the simple expulsion of fakery: not only do illusions 'fool the audience' but they 'are everything the movie can hide behind' (ibid.). The truth then, that Dogme seeks and prioritises, resides in exposure, it removes reassurances, protection: it denies disa-vowal. The truth prevents the normalised or ready processes associated not with filmmaking alone, for far more than filmmaking is being implicated here, but with spectatorship. Yet how do these spirited aims translate into cinema? How do the prime examples, the first and second Dogme films, Thomas Vinterberg's *Festen* (*The Celebration*, 1998) and Lars von Trier's *Idioterne* (*The Idiots*, 1998) manage to unravel illusion, prioritise truth and evade the comforts and conveniences of the classical spectacle?

In a compelling essay Berys Gaut has argued that both films do more than fulfil the Dogme code of practice – they actually work as visual enactments of the Manifesto. They are not just 'instances of the rules and accord with their (main) point' but 'are also *about* the rules and their point' (2003: 93). In other words, the films do not just abide by the imposed constraints on filmmaking, they debate them and the doctrine they mean to express. They are, then, meta-manifestos, as it were: they do Dogme 95 through style, content and intent. However, I want to argue that they are also more specifically meta-manifestos on the ethics of spectatorship. To argue this, we must trace three interrelated issues. Firstly, that the films are indeed *about* the dogma of Dogme. Secondly, that Dogme is, after all, about 'looking on' rather than just making the spectacle, that is, that it is always about spectatorship as well as filmmaking (indeed, the two are far from exclusive realms). Thirdly, that both these necessitate a discussion of ethics.

On the dogma of Dogme

Gaut does a good job paralleling the Manifesto and the style, narrative and agenda of *The Celebration* and *The Idiots*. He shows how both films, through different means, create rule-governed micro-communities that work towards the eruption of truth thereby destabilising the existing oppressive or coercive power structure. Where Gaut comes to focus on the shortfalls and excesses characterising the relationship between Manifesto and films – and other theorists have, similarly, followed this flaws-or-fidelity theme to judge the authenticity of the Dogme product – our concerns are different. I want to bring the discussion of cinema, especially in its illusion-based status and Marxist subtext, back to the notion of agency. In recalling our investigation of cinema as ideology in chapter one and that crucial question that it revolved around – how does the oppressive or coercive system perpetuate itself? How does the illusion pass? – we must ask again, here, why the individual acquiesces, and how Dogme, for example, stages and disturbs this acquiescence.

The Idiots charts the antics of a group of friends who are spending their summer holiday 'spassing': pretending to have mental disabilities or, according to the politically – and provocatively – incorrect film, to be idiots. The group visits various public places to confirm their spassing skills and continue in their search for and appreciation of their 'inner idiot', as Stoffer (Jens Albinus), their would-be leader, terms it. The group members are committed to adhering, and often testing, their capacity to spass. They must find their inner idiot, they must let their truth emerge. That this is a some-what suspect idea – self-indulgent rather than anti-bourgeois – echoes the tongue-in-cheek pomposity of the speedily-written vow of chastity (see Kelly 2000: 5–6). Indeed, Stoffer's self-important attempts to direct the group's war against suburban indifference, whilst idling in an uncle's pseudo-stately home, echoes the arrogance of auteurism (two terms often associated with the anti-auterist von Trier). That is not to say that authority is undermined so much as it is perpetually open to criticism. The directing or command of others is always in evidence but readily undercut: it is one of the central illusions that must be seen to be flawed in order that it can be undone. The spassers are filmed in the rough naturalism of the Dogme directive: the microphone head drops into the top of frames, the camera cannot keep up in the two-shot. This is not naked filmmaking, but, as Gaut suggests, the director 'spassing' (2003: 94). Von Trier, the highly-skilled filmmaker, renders himself 'spectacularly incompetent and deeply ignorant of filmmaking' (ibid.). He becomes one of the characters; in several scenes he interviews the characters/actors in the film's veritably *verité* moments. He joins in. His authority or rather his credibility, and his dislocation from the action, is constantly in question.

Just as 'directing' enters the diegesis, so too does 'acting'. Dogme filmmaking, in its emphasis upon a natural emergence of emotions and elevation of truth, encourages improvisation. In addition to these vox-pop-like interviews, which are interspersed throughout the film, the cast of *The Idiots* were drawn from theatrical backgrounds, thereby supporting a looseness of acting style, the constraint/limitation associated with the free(er) fall of theatre. Improvisation, in dissolving the difference between acting and non-acting, further weakens the bounds between truth and fiction.[5] Just as directing and acting exist in the diegesis, so too, as I will continually emphasise, does spectating. While it is the responsibility of the director that is rendered most explicit within the Dogme 95 Manifesto and the first films, the responsibility of all others involved is always also in evidence. By 'all others', one can distinguish between those providing the spectacle (filmmakers, actors) and those looking on (characters, spec-tators). This distinction is crucial because it represents the breakdown of the conventional oppositions associated with the study of film – between filmmaker and film, and between spectator and film – that rely upon and determine cinema's, and its participants', boundaried states. These conventional distinctions between alienated parties are replaced with a kind of collective complicity that arises from the removal of the buffers separating the previously discrete realms. The Vow of Chastity had laid bare such anti-alienation intent, at least with regard to time and location: 'the film takes place here and now' (Stevenson 2003: 23). *The Idiots* and its provocations are not to be dismissed as extraordinary but, rather, emerge from the everyday. The spectator is not protected by the dislocations or estrangements of foreignness, which arise from setting but also from the supposed sanctity of the different parties' realms.

While, as Gaut states, we are never quite sure of the value of spassing, it is through the character Karen (Bodil Jørgensen) that the spassers' and Dogme's code of conduct come to make sense. I have suggested that spassing works as both deliberate distraction to, as well as tool for, the yielding of truth in these meta-manifestos. Karen's is the truth that emerges from the film. At the holiday's end, Karen returns to her family and, through spassing, shatters the reserve of her husband, and tight-lipped coldness of her family, after the death of their son. She forces herself and her family to confront the awful thing that has happened, dismantling the social conformity they hide behind: their disavowal of empathy and of emotional connectedness. As Gaut puts it: 'by spassing, she forces the truth out of the situation, revealing her grief and anger, and their inability to confront their loss; and she thereby morally condemns them' (2003: 94). But this bid to moral condemnation that Gaut sees happening in this scene has seasoned the entire film. Within the first five minutes of *The Idiots* we are inaugurated into a sphere of spectatorial discomfort, a sphere that characterises or, at the very least, accompanies not only Dogme but contemporary spectatorship in general. This sphere hinges upon, and is enhanced by, the visual emphasis on unearthing the reactions and complicity of those looking on. This is not the stuff of spectatorial surrogacy, but a meditation on the impossibility of innocent bystanding, of positions of neutrality.

Following our introduction to the wide-eyed Karen on her sun-soaked horse-drawn-carriage ride through a leafy lane, we witness an unruly spectacle taking place in the rather austere setting of an expensive restaurant which she enters for lunch. We watch two men with mental disabilities wreaking havoc for the other diners. The diners try to ignore the men: they look down, they stay silent and they pray they will move on. The waiter asks the spassing party to leave. We do not yet know that these men are faking it, so our initial introduction to spassing is as the reaction of others, untempered by our knowledge that these others are being duped. (Of course, the characters are always only acting, but part of our unwritten contract with the film, with any film, is that we suspend such knowledge.) Soon after we will learn that the men were indeed spassing: in the taxi home, they erupt into laughter, shocking Karen who had come with them in 'good faith'. So why this delay? Why wait to reveal their deception? What this delay does is to distract our attention, including, most importantly, our ethical attention, away from the 'truth' and instead focuses on the question of authenticity, on our fascination with the illusion rather than with what it masks. In other words, we get caught up in thinking about how right or wrong it is of the men to fool the diners rather than stay with the more fundamental question of how right or wrong the diners, society's representatives, are in their treatment of people with mental disabilities: the quintessential 'other'. This latter point – the treatment of others – is, I would suggest, the truth of the film and of Dogme, but it has to be played out and emerge from, stop hiding behind, the more comfortable, sensational question of the morality of the spassing. So it does in the final scene when Karen herself uses spassing to trigger her family's true response.

Interestingly, criticism of the film, and writers on Dogme, remain preoccupied with whether the director abides by the rules or not. The ready focus on issues of authenticity (or morality) constantly masks the issue of spectatorial complicity in the illusion. This is the same old story as that surrounding the case of the film *Snuff* in New York in the 1970s. The infamous film, debate and scandal (which concerned whether *Snuff* involved a real murder or not) is the seminal example of the disclaiming of desire through outcry. Linda Williams noted the feminist concern over the appearance of 'snuff' films in 1975 and in particular the feature *Snuff* in 1976: 'the outcry over *Snuff* forced the New York City district attorney to investigate the circumstances of the film's making and to interview the actress who was supposedly killed in the final sequence' (1989: 193).[6] Ultimately it is the actual desire for 'snuff' that is the issue and not the (easily misleading) tension over the verity of the material. The issue of authenticity distracts from and even disavows the individual's desire for the representation of the unseemly and society's investment in it.

Bad taste underpins black humour, perhaps defines it, but the bad taste of 'retard-jokes', or rather the ethical implications, are not consigned to the realm of the reception of *The Idiots* but happen internally, in the film itself. That the characters are 'acting' in spassing (indeed, that the actors are acting as characters acting as 'idiots') stages the ethical issue within the film. By staging it, by having the characters 'acting', ethical negotiation – that is, the discussion of the socially or morally problematic or inappropriate – becomes part of film content and not a knee-jerk reaction to it. This is why the Dogme films are ethical: because they stage the dilemma of implication, and the discomfort of those looking on. What the 'spectators' in *The Idiots* hide behind are each other, and their collusion in *othering* others. Karen is distinguished in her capacity to look at, lock eyes and then hands with the 'other' – she is the only diner in the restaurant to engage with the men, and leaves with them – in contrast to the bystanders at the park and the swimming pool, sites which provide opportunities for spass-testing and comedy, but primarily to stage the reactions and implication of those looking on. Karen's confusion over the group's mission allows an internal airing of the ethical concern mentioned earlier. When she says to Stoffer that the spassers are 'poking fun', who does it really mean that they are poking fun at? We are supposed to think, as Karen indicates, that they are poking fun at 'real people' with mental disabilities, who are, as she unfortunately puts it, 'really ill'. But, again *The Idiots* brings the 'real people' with mental disabilities into the film: a group are hanging out at the house one day when the holiday-makers return home. They are incorporated not only to show that they are obviously not 'ill' but also that they are not the distanced objects of ridicule for post-film accusations of bad taste. Instead, it is those who look on, supposedly innocent, who are the figures of ridicule and for censure.

A similar emphasis upon the dynamics of looking on, of directing, and of participating in the construction of an illusion – so closely aligned with cinema – takes place in *The Celebration*. Vinterberg's film follows the elaborate family celebration for the sixtieth birthday of the wealthy Helge (Henning Moritzen). His close and extended relatives are gathered together at the family's stately hotel for a weekend of celebrations in his honour. In the first speech at dinner his eldest son, Christian (Ulrich Thomsen), regales the party with his childhood tale of how he and his twin sister Linda, who recently committed suicide, were sexually abused as children by their father. The film follows Christian's perseverance in telling his truth, and in finally getting his father to do the same despite the iron-will of social protocol that labels Christian at best disrespectful, at worst 'sick in the head' (Gaut 2003: 95). But there is more to the paralleling of the film and the Manifesto than this outing of the truth.

The illusion that is being challenged, and is finally destroyed, is that of the respectable patriarch, supported by the sophisticated trappings of civility and taste. Like the melange of dramatic strategies comprising the mainstream film, the party represents the skilful harmony of character, music and ceremony all geared to the covering up of the truth and the continuity of the grand event. There is a master of ceremonies (Klaus Bondam), but he is not the obvious director. Christian keeps trying to narrate his own story and Linda will tell hers from beyond the grave. Helge directs the action from a distance, his role both central but masked. To Michael (Thomas Bo Larsen), his youngest and wildest son, Helge delegates the role of editor: Michael must excise or discard the unwanted bits – he and two helpers will twice eject Christian from the room. Michael must also, for his father, keep things running smoothly, seamlessly as it were. Indeed, it is the seamlessness of the spectacle that is being so thoroughly undone here: though the seams reveal not reality but the truth. Michael's rite of passage sees him exercising his own editorial powers: in the final scene he cuts his father out of the family, asking him to leave the room.

What is so important about the meta-cinematic content of the Dogme films for our purposes is that the elevation of truth arises not only from within a dynamic but through the elevation of the collective. Helge removes himself, after Michael's instruction, from the gathering and the 'new order is not an autocracy, but rather a collective and equal society ... The collective replaces the individual autocrat both in the manifesto and in the film' (Gaut 2003: 97). Truth moves from party piece to public declaration: it is confessed to an audience and it is the audience who stifles its import until such stifling is no longer tolerable or conscionable. What makes it intolerable and unconscionable is not simply Christian's pained display, but the anti-collusion momentum from his friends who hide keys, spur him on, staff the spectacle. There is growing discomfort then mild dissent amongst the guests who try to ignore and then try to leave the hotel, but they are allowed to neither simply walk away nor innocently look on. Christian's mother (Birthe Neumann) who attempted both will finally confront her responsibility and cease to collude in her husband's misdeeds. As with *The Idiots*, a climate of collusion, and one that the spectator is an immediate player in, is established at the very start of the film. Within *The Celebration*'s first five minutes we are inaugurated into the discomfort of collusive spectatorship, through the inappropriate acts of others: Michael, who drives by his brother walking to the hotel, throws his wife and kids out of the car so that he can give Christian a lift. Aligned with Christian, but witness to the aggressive and inappropriate behaviour of Michael, our (unconscious) expectations of social conformity are instantly unsettled.

The destruction of the false idol, illusion and elevation of truth is the Dogme manifesto's primary charge. Its other mission is the destruction of the auteurism that underwrites illusion-based cinema. Despite this related charge's striking limitations – Dogme's key directors were both named and famed through Dogme's success – it did effectively emphasise the collective over the singular, and how filmmaking or truth, let's call it 'truthful film', emerges from the group and never solely from the individual.[7] Truthful film, then, does not just oppose bourgeois individualism – as is the common politicised reading of this point of the manifesto – but resides in the interpersonal realm. Truthful film is intersubjective as well as everyday: it comes out of people's connections and responses to each other. Truthful film, then, is implicitly ethical, and it is within an evolving understanding of intersubjectivity that our ethics of spectatorship will finally take shape.

Dogme is meta-cinematic in a different way than *Peeping Tom* and *Strange Days*. It stages spectatorship within its narratives not to promote surrogacy for the ease of spectatorial alignment and pleasure, but to negotiate the responsibility of looking on. *The Celebration* also erodes the distance between the participants (director, actors and characters) in the making of the film. No one singular person orchestrates the action, Vinterberg appears in the film as a taxi driver, and improvisation was incorporated. In discussion with Richard Kelly, Vinterberg claims the extras at the party were not told what Christian was going to confess in his first speech. They had been living together in the house for a couple of weeks prior to shooting, so that they could get to know each other as a family. Their ongoing chatter upon hearing of the child abuse, was their 'natural' response, they 'couldn't really deal with it so they just kept ... talking' (Kelly 2000: 117). *The Celebration*, like *The Idiots*, keeps staging spectating. Again, this is distinct from such meta-cinematic fare as *Rear Window*, precisely because *Rear Window* (like *Strange Days*) sets the spectator centre-stage which is by definition a position never 'hers'. Instead, those looking on in these Dogme films are mainly muted bystanders, defined precisely through their apprehension of and implication in the spectacle. Dogme renders the participants in cinema, from director to spectator, responsible for their presence and contribution and reactions to others.

In a fascinating later film by von Trier, *The Five Obstructions* (2003), he reveals the director as always also in a position of looking on and having to take responsibility and to ethically consider his part in what he is producing. In *The Five Obstructions* von Trier has Jörgen Leth remake five new versions of his 1967 film, *The Perfect Human*, according to various rigid constraints. Where the obstruction for the first remake merely tested and thus confirmed his skill, the second challenged his personal code of conduct and his willingness to submit to von Trier's demands (and the sadomasochistic thrust of their enterprise was not lost on anyone, least of all followers of von Trier's directing style). The second obstruction was the ethical one in that not only did Leth have to re-locate the film to 'the most miserable place on earth', to stage, for example, the eating of a gourmet meal within a context of poverty and depravation, but he had to play the protagonist himself.

In this astonishing scene, Leth confronts the ethical burden of his endeavour, contrasting his self-interests and self-consciousness against the, here literal, backdrop of others. While Leth makes the difficulties of the *dynamic* of looking on explicit, von Trier would 'fail' this remake, for the rules had required that the audience not be seen: the scene was meant to hold the discomforts of directing/spectating without speaking them.

Dogme in general and von Trier in particular stage the impossibility of the neutrality of spectatorship.[8] It is a call to action too: not just for film-makers or for their characters who must act – Christian and Karen must unearth their truths – but for spectators to recognise the complicity of their position. *The Celebration* is all about the father taking responsibility for his actions, and the sons taking responsibility for their lives, and ceasing to participate in the violence of others' actions. Spectatorship, then, is neither to be cosied by the blanket of fantasy, nor animated, temporarily, by the shock of the real, but insistently elbowed by ethical implication. What does this mean exactly? So far ethics has been attached to the idea of a political project described in the Dogme 95 Manifesto, and specifically one that

Fig. 6 *The Five Obstructions*: the ethics of looking on

seeks truth and avoids lies. In other words, one that poses a correct code of conduct and practice for filmmakers and results, supposedly, in a more honest, or open, form of spectatorship. Dictionary definitions of ethics certainly return us to the ethical determination of correct conduct via moral and/or social rules. The discussion of ethics has, understandably, been an ongoing debate within philosophy, which seeks to define both the practice and value of personal conduct, and interrogates what such morally laden, and often subjective, terms as correct and incorrect actually mean. But the ethical register of the Dogme 95 Manifesto resides not simply in its value-laden language, its purism or provocation, nor in its assertion of the social consequences of filmmaking practice, but, most significantly, in its references to response and responsibility within them. It is this sense of ethics that I want to develop in the rest of the chapter.

Towards an ethics of spectatorship

The truth that Dogme so skillfully laid claim to was, as I have suggested, ethically loaded. One may ask if the 'truth' could be anything else in its inevitable reference to honesty and righteousness, and in so asking the critical distinction between ethics and morality opens up before us. This distinction becomes fundamental here for within it lies the all important prioritisation of (ethical) recognition, realisation, reflection – the stuff of agency – over (moral) prescription, proclamation and punishment – the stuff of ideology. In other words ethics, according to Dogme, to countless philosophers, to me, is all about thinking through one's relationship to morality rather than just adhering to it. It is about our personal powers of reasoning and choice when faced with, say, social custom, rather than our complete and immediate accord. It is all about, one could argue, the subject's relationship, imaginary or otherwise, to the conditions of 'his' existence: whether that relationship is characterised by a self-aware consent, even or rather especially within submission, or an instant and unthinking acceptance.

One of the first milestones on our journey towards an ethics of spectatorship, then, is to consider the relationship between ethics and morality in the sphere of cinema, how some films nurture reflection, recognition and responsibility, and some prevent it. In doing so we tie together the different strands of the trip so far, from spectatorial acquiescence (chapter one) to accountability (chapter four), via the pleasures of asserting and relinquishing control (chapters two and three). In scrutinising the morality of our emotional responses, in the analyses of Hollywood's 'moving' pictures below, our overlap with cognitive theories of spectatorial response becomes more apparent. However, where cognitivist theory also privileges the generation of spectators' feelings, our emphasis upon involuntary responses is fervently grounded in unconscious and socio-political processes thereby finding theirs inadequate. Certainly, Murray Smith's delineation of spectators' different levels of engagement – their recognition, alignment and allegiance with characters – provides a very useful sense of the gradated intensities of spectators' experiences (1995: 4). Such gradations have been implicit in my distinction of the different provocative registers of cinema. But where morality and sympathy determine Smith's structuring of these different levels, these terms or regimes of feeling will be shown here to be fundamentally misguiding.

The second milestone is to acknowledge ethics' relationship with its other, but similarly more flamboyant, associate: politics. In doing so, we necessarily move beyond the sealed-off site of cinema to the public sphere. This move is, of course, unavoidable with the relocation of the film spectator to the sofa at home (which though *in* the 'private' realm situates spectatorship within a far wider media stage), and with the relocation of film from the big screen to ever-converging alternative screen medias. We will return to this point later, but for now let us note how this 'turn towards ethics', identified within various critical disciplines, as well as more broadly within the public sphere, has been read by some as a retreat from politics: that invoking the ethical necessarily distracts from the more socially urgent tasks of politicians as well as cultural commentators. As Elizabeth Walden (2002) has noted, this turn also represents the development of a 'savvy professional niche', in which ethical considerations become the jargon *du jour* within various institutions, such as hospitals, social services and universities, as well as a growing trend within critical discourse. However, while morality and ethics are increasingly spoken of, the former functions often at the expense of the latter with both frequently becoming tokenistic or diverting: emptied of social value and impact. Indeed, in the realm of the state, ethics becomes a tool or 'alibi for the heartlessness of right-wing policies'. Walden continues:

> The right's appeal to morality privatises the ethical, employing it tactically in public affairs, in a way that obviates the sort of reflection (about the good, about the good life) that the ethical tradition represents ... Ironically, the appeal to morality functions to clear political discourse of ethical reflection altogether.

This has operated successfully within the neo-liberalism of the presidency of George W. Bush, but is perfectly complemented by New Labour. Tony Blair's hyperbolically earnest appeal to moral integrity, especially in the face of obvious error (over Iraq's weapons), varnished his acts with correctitude: heartfelt humanity overwhelmed, that is, passed for, personal ethics, and, as with Bush, a second term was won despite, or rather because of, previous misdemeanours. In terms of cinema, then, to what extent and effect does Hollywood give shape or story to the spectacle of heartfelt humanity to the exclusion of personal ethics?

Ethics, it seems, currently reclines in a compromised position: in its relative ubiquity within the public sphere, its usefulness for social change and individual responsibility – its agentic charge – has been diminished. It has been 'professionalised' within the workplace: appropriated by due process, integrated into the black hole of good practice. It has also been 'popularised' within state leadership: re-fashioning moralism as the common sense of mass sentiment, staging ethical reflection so no one else need do it. Ethics, then, professionalised and popularised, is sealed off, closed down as a complicating, complicit-ing, agent. How far off this seems from that trilogy of implication – recognition, reflection, responsibility – with which I defined it above. So far off, in fact, that it might protest too much. Might this developing public indulgence in 'ethics', as procedural necessity, earnest alibi and displaced agency, suggest a disavowal?; if this 'public ethics' is a disavowal of sorts, what is it guarding against?

As these popular 'turns' to ethics flourish, a body of ethically-oriented criticism is also emerging which combines philosophical and cultural enquiry with political urgency and personal implication. At its core, frequently, is the writing on ethics by Emmanuel Levinas, a philosopher whose Kantian stance stressed the individual's responsibility, but grounded it in the intersubjective encounter and one predicated on potential violence. Simplifying some of his complex points is, as a short cut, all we can do here, and my aim can only be to set up the richness of his work for the discussion of contemporary spectatorship. First then, Levinas believed that we gain our sense of self only through our face-to-face encounter with the other: our subjectivity is constituted through our response to somebody's difference from us. This response becomes respons-ibility, both as a kind of subjectivity-in-action (a reflexive state of self-constitution) and as our obligation to the other (Levinas 1969; 1981).[9] Such obligation, for Levinas, is not a matter of morality – of empathy or sympathy or reciprocity – but arises from our most primary, and unavoidable, implication in the other's potential death: the murderous impulse that frames self-interest. To put this more simply: my existence necessarily compromises someone else's: it is this ethical dynamic that was perfectly captured in the image from *The Five Obstructions*, of the elegant diner in front of impoverished onlookers, discussed above. As Levinas wrote in his 'Ethics as First Philosophy':

> My being-in-the-world or my 'place in the sun', my being at home, have these not also been the usurpation of spaces belonging to the other man whom I have already oppressed or starved, or driven out into a third world; are they not acts of repulsing, excluding, exiling, stripping, killing? (1989: 82)

The individual's responsibility for the other's 'well-being' – the ethical interconnection between people – is, then, the most important and most primary of principles.

The emphasis upon intersubjectivity made Levinasian thought extremely apt for application to the arts and media which, if they do nothing else, require the individual's encounter with someone beyond themselves. As culture, and the media especially, become increasingly preoccupied with the depiction or debating of the suffering of others, or of the problem of violence – in action films, postmodern fiction, 24-hour news streams – so the need to think through these preoccupations in ethical terms has been highlighted. Joanne Zylinska's *The Ethics of Cultural Studies* (2005) has provided a timely reflection upon the latent ethics of the discipline.[10] But, more than this, film spectatorship – inherently contractual and hooked on the 'real' or imagined suffering of others – does not just appeal to ethical thought but in some ways *is* the ethical encounter. What I mean by this is that spectatorship depends upon our intersubjective alignment with the prospective suffering of others. Indeed, spectatorship, if it is nothing else, is intersubjective. The other's pain is both a commonplace of cinema but also something that we are always implicated in, not only as consumers but as consensual parties in the generation of characters' suffering for our entertainment. Spectatorship is not ethically interesting but intrinsically ethical.

One of the most important writers on the cultural application of Levinas is Judith Butler. She raises key points about the ethics of witnessing the suffering of others in an age of gratuitous violence and re-mediated atrocity, and does so within the specific context of the current political climate. Yet oddly, she ignores the issue of spectatorship. In her work on the ethics of photography in *Precarious Life: The Power of Mourning and Violence* (2004) and her lecture on torture and the Abu Ghraib photographs (2005), Butler thinks through the ethics inherent in the medium – especially its provision of the (Levinasian) 'face' of the other – in order to *de-naturalise* its ideological work, 'to see how dominant forms of representation can and must be disrupted for something about the precariousness of life to be apprehended' (2004: xviii). Of course with Butler's, and before her Susan Sontag's (2003), focus on the dehumanising (and politically expedient) qualities of such war-related photographs, the face of the other is always framed by the racialisation of otherness, something shadowing

Levinas' work too, in his post-Holocaust context. Though Butler acknowledges, indeed concludes her book with, images' rare capacity to move the viewer on from inaction – with how the Vietnam pictures that evaded US censorship fuelled the anti-war movement (2004: 150) – this emotional and aesthetic provocation (not to mention its 'entertainment' value) must be fully explored within the context of spectatorship for the dominant forms of representation to be fully understood and for their disruption to be possible. In the remains of this chapter and the book, I will map out the terrain for the ethics of spectatorship. So far neglected within the growing prioritisation of an ethical study of contemporary culture, spectatorship is, nevertheless, fundamental to its project. As we return our attention to cinema, then, our task is to recast the pleasures of looking on, the suffering being staged and the responses generated, in the alloy of individual agency and social responsibility.

Holy Hollywood: ethics and morality in the sphere of cinema

Cinema, in simple terms, shows us the best and worst ways of being in the world. It does not just instruct us in how to be, say, manly or straight or a mother,[11] but does it frequently through showing us the wrong way to be these things, to embody our identities, our differences from each other. Despite our supposedly secular society in the West, such instructions are saturated with moralism not far removed from their Judeo-Christian roots.

An ethics of spectatorship requires us to think through the moralistic treatment of difference within film. It also requires us to notice the production of indifference in relation to the sentiments that moralistic tracts legitimate. If cinema sets up lines of identification or alignment or allegiance, call it what you will, such lines work to prioritise and universalise the experience of privileged characters, reinforcing the channels of mass sentiment as the wattle and daub of moral-ideological correctitude. However, instead of just attending the creation and crescendo of our feelings in response to specific characteristics, let us also note how this alignment and feeling is fiercely controlled and contained within the text and stops thereafter. At the same time as films produce the extreme emotional expenditure in the name of moral empathy, they also set clear limits to it. There are obvious reasons why this is, among them film's fictional status which will be addressed below. But it is certainly worth asking, especially given the current critical interest in trauma, how the generation of profound emotions by film sits with the necessary forgetting integral to reading/watching entertainment. What is the relationship between spectatorial complicity and complacency in the field of cultural memory?[12]

(i) *The moral and the unethical*
Rather than polarising those films that have a moral framework and those that have not, an ethics of spectatorship directs us instead to think about those films that require us to reflect upon our moral framework and those that do not. As suggested earlier, Dogme stands out as distinctly ethical precisely because it demands this kind of reflection upon our implication in the socially problematic. However, films that lean most heavily on reinforcing moral processes tend to disable the spectators' capacity to engage their own ethical judgements. The films that trace each gradient of the moral high ground to intone the grandeur of their protagonists' actions, be they noble or dastardly, underwrite their moving tales with cast-iron allegiances between the spectator and the tragic but triumphant hero. Rendering the spectator woeful or weepy or merely mesmerised, such visceral reactions, while fuelled by morality, are far from ethical. Just as ethical reflection was connected to recognition of the other, and a taking of responsibility for this recognition and of one's own desires, so such films are unethical precisely because they seem to foreclose recognition and responsibility as well. What do I mean by this? Let us look at some examples of how the moral work of the 'moving' image serves to control or delimit social implication or individual responsibility.

At the end of *Dark Victory* Judith Traherne (Bette Davis), a one-time good-time-girl strikingly reformed since her diagnosis with a fatal illness, goes out with a beatific bang. With her sight having gone – the sign that her end is nigh – she sends her husband away so that she might spare him the agony of witnessing it. She says goodbye to her dogs and takes herself up the wide stairs of her perfect rural haven to her bedroom to expire. The scene clearly depicts the protagonist's heroism, typical of cultural narratives of tragedy (see Stacey 1997: 1–29). The character's self-sacrifice bares all the markers of the denial of the social and physical realities of suffering and death. There is no physical pain, only emotional pain and the emphasis instead is placed on the beauty and martyrdom of death which are accentuated by the celestial music and her climbing the stairs as if ascending to heaven. Such textual strategies are typical of the genre of melodrama, of course. Most importantly, however, the emotivity of the scene underlines how Judith's death marks her fruition as a complete and correct, that is married and selfless, woman in sharp contrast to her previous ways. Melodramatic morality operates through the rigid dictation of spectatorial emotion that underwrites its ideological terms with a righteous righting of previous wrongs.

Turning to contemporary director Steven Spielberg, we find other highly moving but far more socially invested depictions of human suffering. Indeed, Spielberg trades more than most on the momentousness of mass sentiment. Despite his near habitual interest in atrocity – genocide (*Schindler's List*, 1993), slavery (*Amistad*, 1997) and, most recently, armageddon (*War of the Worlds*, 2005) – it was only with *Saving Private Ryan* (1998) that Spielberg was found to finally engage in 'a long painful look at the face of human death' (Arthur 2001: 354 n.26). How is this painful look achieved, and what response does it produce in the spectator? Let us look more closely at one of his, arguably one of the, most 'powerful' and 'moving' film sequences from recent cinema history. Spielberg's record-breakingly long sequence of the Normandy D-Day landings certainly seems to provide the slow deliberate recognition of, reflection upon and responsibility for, the death of the other. Certainly its prolonged and pronounced confrontation with the banal horror of soldiers falling, losing their limbs, wits or consciousness, presented suffering as it had not been presented before. Though Spielberg accentuates the visual pleasures of rubbernecking in his indulgence in the spectacle of suffering, he also includes major impediments to this pleasure within this scene. There are literal impediments to vision such as the objects, bodies, smoke and water that block the view, but also the non-literal impediments such as the horror, the enormity of the event being captured, the relentlessness of the length and content (and virtuosity)[13] of the scene. Where normally the spectator is aligned with an on-screen suffering character who tells us how to react and to feel about what is going on (think Shirley MacLaine's character in *Terms of Endearment* (1983) waxing hysterical about her daughter's pain), in *Saving Private Ryan*, Tom Hanks's character, Miller, lacks emotional response. In fact, he is distinctly de-privileged as on-screen witness. Instead the heightened subjectivity that is created on-screen belongs to the scene: the restless movement between various points of view – the longer takes down the firing machine guns, the fast-paced hand-held disembodied filming from within the water – none of which seem 'owned' by single characters but by the historical event itself and fortified by stylistic reference to documentary as well as Robert Capa's photographs (1944).

The scene does not just stage death on a grand scale, but moves the spectator through its epic proportions. It is all about moving the spectator: not punishing the spectator for looking but making punishment part of the gift of looking. Not only does this square with that previously identified as the masochistic impulse of spectatorship – the pleasure of assimilating others' pain – but begs the question of masochism's relationship to ethics. The spectator's reaction is channelled into a heavily subjective but explicitly visceral experience defined by some form of suffering. The giddy point-of-view shots imitate Miller's increasing disorientation; the muted sound imitates shellshock. It is not the *mise-en-scène*, not the description of the scene, but the specifically cinematic qualities that move the spectator. That Miller is 'numbed' instead of us, that he owns a lack of feeling, prohibits it from being our response, despite the jadedness that readily informs contemporary spectatorship, accentuating instead the power of what we are not just looking at but experiencing.

So the spectator is most definitely moved and even implicated in the scene, but being moved, I want to argue, marks the experience as moral but not ethical: involuntary emotion is the opposite of reflection and implication. The scene does well to avow a range of realities of death and suffering, but in so doing it perpetuates an enduring form of the denial of other's suffering. Let us now call this denial what it is: spectatorial insulation. It does this precisely through moving the spectator. It is the very power of the spectacle and its moral impact that provokes but also limits the experience. As Franco Moretti said of 'moving literature', our tears or our involuntary reactions to provocative images are exactly what keep us at a distance from them. They strengthen our removal as 'a ritual of reciprocal collective absolution' (1983: 173). We cry, gasp or grimace and in so doing we acquit ourselves of our part in the production of and indulgence in the pain of others. Our insulation from responsibility is underwritten by the shared-ness of the response. How different these *collective* involuntary reactions are to the intimacy of the spectator's turned-on-ness discussed in the last chapter. Moretti goes on to proclaim these tears 'a catharsis that implies a definite disavowal of the tragic' (ibid.). These involuntary or visceral reactions symbolise a requisite, defensive denial of the profundity or implications of the representation. The issue is not whether we are denying death, of ourselves or of others, but rather that we are denying our part in what we are watching: our desire to witness it (through film), know of it (through media) or support it (through politics). As Sontag said of highly moving photographs of atrocity:

> And it is not necessarily better to be moved. Sentimentality, notoriously, is entirely compatible with a taste for brutality and worse ... The imaginary proximity to the suffering inflicted on others that is granted by images suggests a link between the faraway sufferers – seen in close-up on the television screen – and the privileged viewer that is simply untrue, that is yet one more mystification of our real relations to power. So far as we feel sympathy, we feel we are not accomplices to what caused the suffering. Our sympathy proclaims our innocence as well as our importance. (2003: 91–2)

When we are moved, especially at the horrors of war or at the horrors of illness, we are not taking responsibility for these horrors not happening again but quite the opposite, we are absolving ourselves of responsibility. Our 'tears' are 'our bit' – they show we are able to recognise what is awful or wrong but that is usually all. The powerfully emotive moral register of *Saving Private Ryan* dictates our strong feelings about such representations. It guarantees our response, but as guarantee – as one-sided, conditional claim – its absolutist, moral terms are in opposition with the ethical contract discussed earlier.

(ii) *the ethical and the immoral*
To what extent is an awareness of ethical reflection and responsibility possible in the absence of a moral framework? I argued above that a film that is morally invested is not necessarily ethically invested. But is a film that is morally deficient not necessarily unethical? Can a film that defies or simply ignores morality – is immoral or amoral – still invite ethical spectatorship? Dogme is, in many ways, amoral cinema, and it is ethical because of it: it renders morality irrelevant in its ethical emphases. Indeed amorality – as the absence of interest in or deference to morality – could be seen as an essential ingredient to ethical cinema. In contrast, films' immorality

– as the evident transgression or corruption of moral rules – can still invoke (the ethical deficiency of) moral spectatorship. Such films draw forth the moral frameworks of the audience because of their absence from the text. This moral spectatorship privileges, and is distracted by, the dangers of the immoral film and sets its limit there. As such, it disavows the social and libidinal implications of seemingly immoral films – as *Basic Instinct* or *Peeping Tom* or *Funny Games* (1997) were sometimes labelled – thereby, as suggested previously, denying what we could now call their truth: the spectatorial desires (be it masochism, or perversity) that they cater to. Further, I would argue that for a film to be immoral is near impossible: films cannot refute morality, for, as Smith illustrated, it is always part of the 'co-text' of spectatorship: the set of social mores and moral values that spectators bring with them (1995: 194). It is worth emphasising that this 'set' is not sealed but very much in process, triggered by the exchanges between textual content, unconscious processes and the collective impressions of the public audience.

Dogme is not alone in its moral indifference. I would like to point to two other branches of contemporary anti-moral cinema, both of which have been distinguished for their excesses and violent content, indeed for their postmodernism, which, in diminishing agency, has been deemed unethical (Slack & Whitt 1992: 581–2). The first branch readily connects to the self-reflexive trajectory mentioned earlier, and the examples that leap out in their intense meta-cinematicism and moral bankruptcy are *Funny Games*, *Henry: Portrait of a Serial Killer* (1986) and *Man Bites Dog* (1992). Each of these art-house films traces the random, graphic, murders of serial killers. Not only do they speak to the cultural fascinations of our 'age of sex crime' (Caputi 1988), but fervently implicate the spectator in its perpetuation. Henry will film his murders to watch them later. The killer in *Man Bites Dog* is accompanied by a film crew who are making a documentary about him. In *Funny Games*, as well as the murderous protagonist's direct address to the spectator, at one point he picks up a remote control and the scene rewinds before us in a quintessentially 'contract-breaking' move. What J. Hoberman said of *Funny Games*, that it aggressively aims 'to implicate the viewer in the spectacle of violent cruelty' (1998: 59), is equally true of the other films. These examples are contra-disavowal also in their characters' banal enactment of extreme brutality which defamiliarises the spectators' experience, denying them any insulation from the most unconscionable of acts. Yet the unconscious is at the root of the unconscionable, and the spectators' investments and desires are always, if not especially, implicated in it. These films sit within a wave of viscerally-provocative, mostly European cinema, and one that can be seen as a by-product of the clean-up of Hollywood post-Clinton (Helmore 2003; Williams 2005: 37). Haneke's work certainly continues its characteristics: his 2000 film *Code Unknown* is a fascinating look at the complicity of those looking on and the problematic of by-standing.

The other branch of anti-moral cinema lies within independent film-making in North America and is comprised of the postmodernist hyperbole and interpretational vacuity of such films as *Kill Bill: Vol. I* (2003), *Kill Bill: Vol. II* (2004) and *Sin City* (2005). So astonishingly empty of provocation and emotivity are they that they can but make us more aware of the exploitation of our feelings in other movies. These films, let us take *Sin City* as the prime example, are also the polar opposites of Dogme 95. They represent the antithesis of its manifesto. Rather than privilege truth, they lie at endless (Platonic) removes from the original. They are adaptations, frequently of cartoons or, at least, drawing on cartoon aesthetics to heighten their aura of artificiality in their flamboyant violence and locations. *Sin City*, as well as referencing Frank Miller's comic books on which it was based, also alludes to other films through casting and characterisation: Clive Owen's character, for example, both alludes to and pokes fun at his previous role in *King Arthur* (2004). The films are thoroughly indulgent of the spectacle and its cosmetics with excessive use of make-up, special effects and even prosthetics. Far from privileging community and intersubjectivity *Sin City*, instead, tells of lone heroes in a non-linear narrative. A heavily edited genre-extravaganza, its parodic intertextuality references *noir*, superheroes, gross-out comedy, action films and even melodrama. Despite allowing characters to express their sadness, or regret, *Sin City* is thoroughly anti-sentimental: the emotional expressions are resonance-less. Indeed the film defies both the spectator's will to identify and any 'structure of sympathy' (Smith 1995: 85) to be rendered, somehow, beyond morality.

So where does all of this leave us? An ethics of spectatorship requires us to think about how we are positioned, and interpellated, with regard to the morality, immorality or amorality of film. It does not just acknowledge how we consent to our submission to the spectacle, but asks us to consider how we are rendered accountable or not to what we have consented to, and part of the contract of spectatorship, of course, is that we do not renege on the deal. It asks many more questions too. Does the film depict or enact justice? Does it render suffering as alien, intimate, emotive or implicating? What does it mean for a film to be unconscionable, rather than about the unconscionable, to reinforce or overstep the boundaries of acceptability or good taste? And who sets these boundaries?

At the start of this chapter I distinguished two ways in which cinema has historically evaded ethical reflection: through its moral frameworks and its fiction status. We have done morality to death, and so to the final frontier. Film, no matter how true to life it seems in its themes, characterisations or the vividness of its images, or how reprehensible, perverse, gratuitous or unseemly it feels, is not real. It is a cultural artefact, a representation-based form of entertainment. Far from being the ultimate limiting factor to a politics of spectatorship, in these, the book's, concluding moments I will suggest that the exchange between film culture, spectatorial response and reality is ethically entangled and socially pressing.

Conclusion: regarding (un)real suffering

So inured are we to the staging of others' suffering, that we do not think twice about Hollywood's graphic offerings. The summer blockbuster of 2005, *The Fantastic Four*, banked on audiences' thrill at viewing carnage in New York again: the sublime spectacle of the detailed destruction of a beloved object. Yet in the immediate wake of 9/11 *Collateral Damage* (2002), an Arnold Schwarzenegger movie about terrorist attacks on New York, was pulled from release in the States. A week after the 7 July 2005 London bombings, Channel 5 in the UK pulled the Quentin Tarantino-directed episode of *CSI: Crime Scene Investigation* because of its subject matter.[14] Cultural commentators and screen theorists alike have written of the decreasing distance between the spectacle and the real (see King 2005). This is pinned to two things. On one side is the similarity between fictional image content and the news: so that, for example, those viewing the destruction of the twin towers of the World Trade Center could state that it 'was like a movie'. And on the other is the similarity between news content and the tropes of fiction: how the mediation of suffering neces-sarily incurs entertainment values associated with narrativity, emotivity and visual pleasure. What both amount to is how the spectacle and the real can look alike, and therefore need to be analysed, at times, through similar terms. Just as social theories have had to be applied to the study of film and television, so spectatorship theory – the understanding of how those looking on take meaning or pleasure or comfort or distance from what they see – needs to be applied to the study of society and its current affairs.

For several theorists there can be no richer site for ethical consideration – that is, for our encounter with the other by way of 'his' pain – than the photographs of real suffering generated, for example, by 'at-the-front' journalism. These photographs occupy the fascinating medial point between the regimes of art and those of the news, between the spectacle and the real. Sontag's work has been central here. Her 1977 book *On Photography* and her last book *Regarding the Pain of Others* (2005) consider how 'our culture of spectatorship neutralises the moral force of photographs of atrocities' (2005: 94). Such photographs can be both powerfully provocative and numbing, they can conjure the 'mystery, and the indecency, of [our] co-spectatorship' (2005: 53) or the 'beauty in ruins' (2005: 67). In other words, such photographs must be framed, although she does not say so explicitly, by the complex and alluring tension between witnessing violence and being in some way entertained by it. It is this tension, this dialectical relationship between the socially or personally problematic and the individual's desires, that has underwritten my study. And it is its troubling implications that were being 'managed' by the various distancing devices or processes of disavowal that we revealed. Such processes, which operated across the text-context-psyche expanse, worked to insulate those looking on from any ethical repercussions. What I have been arguing in this chapter is that spectatorship is under new management, and ignoring its latent ethics is untenable.

So what of cinema, then, that asks us to look not at real suffering but at suffering posing as real? That asks us not to witness the pain of others, but to watch that pain being inflicted, and to require that that pain be inflicted for our entertainment. Watching real and fabricated suffering is different only in so much as the spectator's involuntary response to such scenes has been framed by opposing kinds of foreknowledge. In watching the news, we come with the expectation that it is 'true', in watching an action film, we come with the expectation that it is 'fiction'. As we see more and more real suffering in our real lives, what are we to make of all the fabricated real suffering we have been watching for years? The crucial point here is not to get hung up on the 'is it real?' and 'dismiss it if it isn't' issue – as if only real things are meaningful – but to interrogate the real or fiction status of images of suffering for their impact upon questions of personal and social response and responsibility. (The fake photographs of British soldiers abusing Iraqi prisoners in the wake of the Abu Ghraib scandal provides a fascinating example here, not only because of the ease with which such abuse was deemed likely by the British public, but by the market for these images that these photographs fed). I am not in any way trying to level the experience of seeing blood spurting from severed limbs in a war film and seeing the limbless corpses of the aftermath of a suicide bomber in a CNN report – it matters very much that some acts really happened – but to recognise the importance of placing them, albeit at either ends, of some kind of continuum of spectatorship.

This continuum of spectatorship spans not only the fiction/non-fiction divide, but the formerly boundaried sites of different screen media. To the two reasons for the decreasing distance between the spectacle and the real must be added a third: location. The spectacle invades the real, and vice versa, because they have ceased to occupy exclusive realms. While it was 'necessarily in a crowd that one finds the cinematic spectator' (Shwartz 1995: 316) this is only part of the story now. With the ascension of sofa spectatorship, regarding the real and unreal suffering of others (in the facts of news and the fictions of movies) now takes place in exactly the same space, the home, and invariably on the same screen. Of course this is not the first time that news and movies have co-habited: newsreels were a constant presence in theatres from early cinema until television rendered them redundant in the 1960s. What is critical now, however, is more than their common content, aesthetics and entertainment values: their privatisation. Film spectatorship has been domesticated and personalised, though this might imply its removal from socio-political tensions (from, for example, the collective rituals, social mores, sexual embarrassments of the public theatre) and hence a decommissioning of disavowal, or of ethical implication, this is far from the case. Instead, as argued in chapter three, the explosion of the home video market, which turned sexual cinema, in particular, into a domestic leisure activity, was situated within a pronounced social play-off between the indulgence in and segregation of 'perversity'. And, as shown in this chapter, the ethics of spectatorship is a necessary by-product of both contemporary and postmodern filmmaking, and of the convergence of media, of practices of looking on.

The seismic shift in the nature of spectatorship, noted in the previous chapter with reference to the VCR, has continued, then, with the development and dominance of digital media. Spectatorship has moved beyond the cinema auditorium (where exhibition now functions partly as pre-sell for the DVD), to be characterised by portability and interactivity. Films are bought and borrowed, dipped into or dwelt on, watched and re-watched on trains, planes and even automobiles. The busy-ness and business of contemporary spectatorship seems light years away from the passivity of the 'classical' set up, especially as it was perceived by 1970s film theory. In her latest work, Laura Mulvey acknowledges the radical transformation of spectatorship by new media technologies, yet still seems to locate her 'pensive' or 'possessive' spectator within an albeit revamped version of the sadistic model (2005). What this book has argued, in contrast, is that transformations in spectatorship (resulting from both technological and social practices) maintain and enhance the masochistic economy underwriting spectatorship: film is still all about the pleasure of unpleasure, yet our indulgence in it remains remote but controllable.

NOTES

Chapter one

1   For a discussion of the cultural interpretations of May 1968 see Reader (1993). Richard Allen claimed that the trigger to radical theory was the events' failure to 'provoke radical social change' (1995: 7), while Philip Rosen suggests that the events were the crystallisation of existing 'political-cultural impulses' (1986: 10).

2   Figureheads of French thought, and indeed of Structuralism, lent their support to the social unrest. Lacan was rumoured to have smuggled the student leader, Daniel Cohn-Bendit, back into France following his deportation (Reader 1993: 14).

3   Unless of course it is her ceiling.

4   In his essay 'Freud and Lacan', also in *Lenin and Philosophy*, Althusser is more explicit about misrecognition and its place within ISAs (1971: 189–220).

5   Her distinction between the visual image's active male and passive female restated and built upon the earlier work of John Berger (1972).

6   These theorists were distinguishing between mainstream, dominant forms of texts (novels) and more oppositional narratives that did not conceal themselves as discourse. Barthes' distinction of writerly and readerly texts was part of this politicised project (see Barthes 1974: 4).

Chapter two

1   For a useful discussion of Hitchcock's films and cinematography, see http://www. rottentomatoes.com/vine/showthread.php?t=416465&page=5.

2   She does this much to the chagrin of several theorists, D. N. Rodowick (1991) for one who finds the slippage from the pre-sexualisation of the phase to it being clearly gendered, extremely problematic.

3   Much of the critical work on *noir* attends its status as genre or mood or style, thus one can query its categorisation through scare quotes.

4   For an extensive discussion of this film and its sexual politics, see Michele Aaron, 'The Blunt Cutting Edge: Taking the Knife to the *Body of Evidence*', in Deborah Cartmell, Ian Hunter and Heidi Kaye (eds) *Sisterhoods: Feminists in Film and Fiction* (London: Pluto Press, 1998).

5   See Madonna, *Sex* (New York: Warner Books, 1992).

6   For Mulvey, only a counter-cinema could operate outside of the binary laws of sexual difference underwriting the ideological workings of patriarchy. Other feminists would see the potential of television as an alternative site. *L'Ecriture Feminine*, which called on women to write through the body, through their experiences, to oppose patriarchy, was proposed by Hélène Cixous in her 1976 essay 'The Laugh of the Medusa' (1981: 245–64).

7   'The association of tears and "wet wasted afternoons" (in Molly Haskell's words (1974: 154)) with genres specified as feminine (the soap opera, the "woman's picture") points very precisely to this type of over-identification, this abolition of a distance, in short, this inability to fetishise' (Doane 1991: 23–4).

8   In that it was a process comprised of various stages of assimilation of the other, such as recognition and adoption.

9   Other audience studies followed. See also Richard Dyer (1981); Dorothy Hobson (1982); Ien Ang (1985); David Buckingham (1987); Christine Geraghty (1991).

Chapter three

1   Freud has also read the 'gone' as a vengeful reaction to the mother's leaving him, and the child's compensation for 'his' lack of complaint at her departure. See Freud 1991a: 285.

2   For discussions of the characteristics of *noir*, see Tuska 1984: xxi–iv; Krutnik 1991: x–xii; Silver & Ursini 1996; Bould 2005.

3   The film grossed $352.7m worldwide, and $53m in rentals in the US. It received Academy Award and Golden Globe nominations; Sharon Stone, however, won two MTV awards, for best female performance and most desirable female.

4   Some of the noirish films of the 1970s and 1980s would 'shift genre identities to trade on the new term when re-released' (L. R. Williams 2005: 3)

5   For a discussion of the active role of women in film noir in front of and behind the camera, see Cowie 1993.

6   Susie Bright, renowned 'sexpert' and queer writer, also appeared in a cameo in the film.

7   Dino De Laurentiis films are often associated with both commercial success and sensationalism or crassness.

8   *Bodily Harm* (James Lemmo, 1995), a straight-to-video film starring Linda Fiorentino and Daniel Baldwin which repeats in reverse *Basic Instinct*, is a perfect example of the problems attending female masochism and a male murderer. Catherine

Tramell's reincarnation as Sam Keen might promise the quintessential male sexual killer, but this paradigm cannot be simply inverted for it is so loaded: Sam is hardly punished for the sadistic murders and a framed female dies in his place. *Bodily Harm* is far from being an accomplished film, but is a telling reflection of the spectre of gender in the 1990s eroticisation of death.

9   The late 1990s witnessed a spate of disaster-oriented films such as *Outbreak* (Wolfgang Peterson, 1995), *Dante's Peak* (Roger Donaldson, 1997), *Volcano* (Mick Jackson, 1997), *Armageddon* (Michael Bay, 1998), *Deep Impact* (Mimi Leder, 1998) and so on, which like the proliferation of blockbuster horror and neo-*noir* is commonly attributed to technological developments and pre-millennial anxieties.

10   For a discussion of body modification see Myers 1992; Curry 1993; Sweetman 1999.

11   See also Scott 1983.

12   For a discussion of neo-*noir* see Erickson 1996.

13   See Deleuze 1991; Massé 1992; Silverman 1992; Thompson 1994; Fitzpatrick Hanly 1995; Siegel 1995; Mansfield 1997; Noyes 1997; Hart 1998; Phillips 1998; Savran 1998; Stewart 1998.

14   Soft- and hard-core, gay and straight sex films (pornographic films intended only for the viewer's sexual stimulation) often use sadomasochistic imagery to enhance their provocation. They incorporate the accoutrements of S&M – leather, PVC, whips, handcuffs, and so on – to 'spice up' the spectacle, but, as Tanya Krzywinska (2005) points out in her investigation of the genre of Explicit Sex Films, while much feminist analysis might suggest otherwise, B&D (Bondage & Discipline, which exploits S&M) is not the most prevalent type of porn and these 'exotic' acts ultimately support a conservatism implicit to the genre.

15   The retail market for DVDs frequently exceeds monies generated from box office takings, a point made by several contributors to the 'What is a DVD?' conference held at Warwick University, 23 April 2005.

16   For the heated debates on Hutchence's cause of death see the British press during February and March 1998. In 1991, Grace Jones would claim that 'auto-erotic asphyxiation is pretty hot ... I've been dabbling' (qouted in Lermer 1991: 75). Patricia Cornwell's *The Body Farm* was noted for its 'Milliganesque sexual practices' in *Gay Times* (Anon. 1995a: 76). The same magazine commented that a Guinness advertisement in 1997 which 'depict[ed] a masked, leather-and-rubber-clad Tory hanging by his neck next to a bowl of oranges' had 'not surprisingly, outraged the Conservative Party' (Anon. 1997: 40).

17   Patricia Bosworth states that 'the FBI estimates that from five hundred to one thousand such deaths occur each year' (1985: 54).

18   'Lesbians and Gay Men in the US Military: Historical Background'; On-line. Available at http://psychology.ucdavis.edu/rainbow/html/military_history.html (accessed 12 October).

19 There is an important, and fascinating, future discussion to be had about sofa spectatorship and masochism in the light of such programmes as *Jackass* and *Dirty Sanchez* and their spinoffs, especially in terms of how class might function as distancing device. I am more than grateful to Samantha Dawkins for this point.

Chapter 4

1 This section is an adaptation of my article 'Looking On: Troubling Spectacles and the Complicitous Spectator' in King 2004.

2 In this genre, self-reflexivity operates on two main fronts: through spectacles (the overt artificiality or staged-ness of the musical numbers with their non-diegetic orchestral accompaniments) and through their frequent depiction of putting on a show, most commonly in the Backstage Musicals.

3 This has proven particularly prevalent in recent cycles of postmodern horror films.

4 For the connection between Brecht and psychoanalytic disavowal, see Heath 1974.

5 This is also made evident in Saul Metzstein's 2000 film on the Dogme 'Brotherhood' for Channel 4 Television, *The Name of this Film is Dogme 95*. This film was based on Richard Kelly's book of the same year.

6 Williams makes reference to an article in the *New York Times*, 10 March 1976. David Kerekes and David Slater have argued that 'the *filming* of a killing would seem a greater atrocity than the act of murder itself' (1994: vii, emphasis in original).

7 The first charge is flawed too: there is editing and aesthetics in the films.

8 Von Trier's *Dancer in the Dark* (2000) and Susanne Bier and Anders Thomas Jensen's *Open Hearts* (2002), especially, are similarly preoccupied with the discomfort and implication of looking on.

9 I am grateful to Anat Pick for helping me clarify this dual definition.

10 See also Davis 2004; Valier and Lippens 2004; Cooper 2006.

11 Or, in the case of *Mr Mom* (Stan Dragoti, 1983), all three.

12 For an interesting though unconnected discussion of an afterwards of spectatorship see Sutton 1999: 80.

13 I am grateful to Catherine Grant for this point.

14 Though how many more tuned in the next week as a result, or subsequently bought the special release DVD of his two-part episode?

BIBLIOGRAPHY

Aaron, Michele (1994) 'Comings and Goings: The Female Sexual Killer in Contemporary Cinema', unpublished MA thesis, Southampton University.

____ (1998) 'The Exploits of the Female Sexual Killer: Taking the Knife to the *Body of Evidence*', in Deborah Cartmell, I. Q. Hunter, Heidi Kaye and Imelda Whelehan (eds) *Sisterhoods: Acfoss the Literature/Media Divide*. London: Pluto Press, 167–82.

____ (1999) 'Introduction', in Michele Aaron (ed.) *The Body's Perilous Pleasures: Dangerous Desires and Contemporary Culture*. Edinburgh: Edinburgh University Press, 1–10.

____ (2000) 'Un/Safe Texts: "Madmen", Masochists and the Representation of Self-endangerment', unpublished PhD thesis, Southampton University.

____ (2004) 'Looking On: Troubling Spectacles and the Complicitous Spectator', in Geoff King (ed.) *The Spectacle of the Real: From Hollywood to Reality TV and Beyond*. Exeter: Intellect, 213–22.

Abrams, M. H. (1981) *Glossary of Literary Terms*. London: Holt, Rinehart and Winston.

Allen, Richard (1995) *Projecting Illusion: Film Spectatorship and the Impression of Reality*. New York: Cambridge University Press.

Althusser, Louis (1971 [1969]) 'Ideology and Ideological State Apparatuses: Notes towards an Investigation', in *Lenin and Philosophy*, trans. Ben Brewster. New York: Monthly Review Press.

Altman, Rick (ed.) *Genre: The Musical*. London: British Film Institute.

Ang, Ien (1985) *Watching Dallas: Soap Opera and the Melodramatic Imagination*. London: Methuen.

Anon. (1994) 'Rough Sex Led to Boy's Death, Officer Says', *New York Times*, 19 July, B4.

____ (1995a) 'Review of Patricia Cornwell's *The Body Farm*', *Gay Times*, February, 76.

____ (1995b) Untitled article, *The Guardian*, 1 March, 12.

____ (1997) 'Guinness Drops Kinky Tory advertisement', *Gay Times*, February, 40.

Arroyo, José (1993) 'Death, Desire and Identity: The Political Unconscious of "New Queer Cinema"', in Joseph Bristow and Angelia R. Wilson (eds) *Activating Theory: Lesbian, Gay, Bisexual Politics*. London: Lawrence & Wishart, 70–96.

Arthur, Paul (2001) 'The Four Last Things: History, Technology, Hollywood, Apocalypse', in Jon Lewis (ed.) *The End of Cinema as We Know It: American Film in the Nineties*. New York: New York University Press, 342–55.

Austin, Thomas (1999) 'Desperate to see it: Straight men watching *Basic Instinct*' in Melvyn Stokes and Richard Maltby (eds) *Identifying Hollywood's Audiences: Cultural Identity and the Movies*. London: British Film Institute

Barthes, Roland (1974 [1970]) *S/Z*, trans. Richard Miller. New York: Hill & Wang.

_____ (1981) 'Theory of the Text', in Robert Young (ed.) *Untying the Text*. London: Routledge and Kegan Paul, 31–47.

'*Basic Instinct*: Awards and Nominations', *The International Movie Database*, On-Line. Available HTTP: http://us.imdb.com (10 Dec. 1999)

Baudry, Jean-Louis (1985 [1970]) 'Ideological Effects of the Basic Cinematographic Apparatus', in Bill Nicholls (ed.) *Movies and Methods Volume II: An Anthology*. Berkeley: University of California Press, 531–42.

_____ (1986 [1975]) 'The Apparatus: Metaphysical Approaches to the Impression of Reality in the Cinema', in Philip Rosen (ed.) *Narrative, Apparatus, Ideology: A Film Theory Reader*. New York: Columbia University Press, 56–71.

Becker, Ernest (1973) *The Denial of Death*. New York: The Free Press.

Bellour, Raymond (1979) 'Alternation, Segmentation, Hypnosis: Interview with Raymond Bellour', interview by Janet Bergstrom, *Camera Obscura*, 3–4, Summer, 93.

Benveniste, Emile (1971) *Problems in General Linguistics*, trans. Mary Meek. Coral Gables, MI: University of Miami Press.

Berger, John (1972) *Ways of Seeing*. Harmondsworth: Penguin.

Bergstrom, Janet (1990 [1979]) 'Enunciation and sexual difference', in Constanace Penley (ed.) *Feminism and Film Theory*. New York: Routledge, 159–185.

Bernard, Oliver (1989) *The Finger Points at the Moon: Inscriptions from Paris, May 1968*. London: Tuba Press.

Blau, Melinda (1994) 'Ordinary People', *New York*, 28 November, 38–46.

Bobo, Jacqueline (1988) '*The Color Purple*: Black Women as Cultural Readers', in E. Deidre Pribram (ed.) *Female Spectators: Looking at Film and Television*. London: Verso, 90–109.

Booth, Wayne (1988) 'Who is Responsible in Ethical Criticism, and for What?', *The Company We Keep: An Ethics of Fiction*. Berkeley: University of California Press, 125–55.

Bosworth, Patricia (1985) 'Let's Call It Suicide', *Vanity Fair*, March, 54.

Bould, Mark (2005) *Film Noir: From Berlin to Sin City*. London: Wallflower Press.

Bronfen, Elizabeth (2004) 'Femme Fatale – Negotiations of Tragic Desire', *New Literary History*, 35, 2, 103–17.

Browne, Nick (1986) 'The Spectator-in-the-Text: The Rhetoric of *Stagecoach*', in Philip Rosen (ed.) *Narrative, Apparatus, Ideology: A Film Theory Reader*. New York: Columbia University Press, 102–19.

Brundson, Charlotte (ed.) (1986) *Films for Women*. London: British Film Institute.

Buckingham, David (1987): *Public Secrets: Eastenders and its Audience*. London: British Film Institute.

Butler, Judith (2004) *Precarious Life: The Power of Mourning and Violence*. London: Verso.

____ (2005) 'Torture and the Ethics of Photography', Centre for Research in Philosophy and Literature Seminar, Warwick University, 24 May.

Caputi, Jane (1988) *The Age of Sex Crime*. London: The Women's Press.

Chancer, Lynn S. (1992) *Sadomasochism in Everyday Life: The Dynamics of Power and Powerlessness*. New Brunswick, NJ: Rutgers University Press.

Cixous, Hélène (1981 [1976]) 'The Laugh of the Medusa', in Elaine Marks and Isabelle de Courtivron (eds) *New French Feminisms: An Anthology*. Brighton: Harvester Press, 245–64.

Clover, Carol (1992) *Men, Women and Chainsaws: Gender in the Modern Horror Film*. Princeton, NJ: Princeton University Press.

Comolli, Jean-Louis (1980) 'Machines of the Visible', in Teresa de Lauretis and Stephen Heath (eds) *The Cinematic Apparatus*. London: Macmillan, 121–43.

Cook, Pam and Claire Johnston (1990 [1974]) 'The Place of Woman in the Cinema of Raoul Walsh', in Patricia Erens (ed.) *Issues in Feminist Film Criticism*. Bloomington: Indiana University Press, 19–27.

Cook, Pam and Mieke Bernink (eds) (1999) *The Cinema Book*, second edition. London: British Film Institute.

Cooper, Sarah (2006) *Selfless Cinema?: Ethics and French Documentary*. Oxford: Legenda.

Cowie, Elizabeth (1979/80) 'The Popular Film as Progressive Text – a discussion of *Coma*', part I, *m/f*, 3, 1979, 59–82; part 2 *m/f*, 4, 1980, 57–69.

____ (1984) 'Fantasia', *m/f*, 9, 71–104.

____ (1993) '*Film Noir* and Women', in Joan Copjec (ed.) *Shades of Noir: A Reader*. London: Verso, 121–65.

____ (1997) *Representing the Woman: Psychoanalysis and Cinema*. London: Macmillan/ Minneapolis: Minnesota University Press.

Culler, Jonathan (1975) *Structuralist Poetics: Structuralism, Linguistics and the Study of the Literature*. Ithaca: Cornell University Press.

Curry, D. (1993) 'Decorating the Body Politic', *New Formations*, 19, 69–82.

Davis, Therese (2004) *The Face on the Screen: Death, Recognition & Spectatorship*. Bristol: Intellect.

Dayan, Daniel (1976) 'The Tutor-Code of Classical Cinema', in Bill Nicholls (ed.) *Movies and Methods Volume I*. Berkeley: University of California Press, 438–51.

de Lauretis, Teresa (1984) *Alice Doesn't: Feminism, Semiotics, Cinema*. Bloom-ington: Indiana University Press.

____ (1999 [1985]) 'Oedipus Interruptus', in Sue Thornham (ed.) *Feminist Film Theory: A Reader*. Edinburgh: Edinburgh University Press, 83–96.

de Saussure, Ferdinand (1966 [1915]) *Course in General Linguistics*. London: Mc-Graw-Hill.

Deleuze, Gilles (1991) *Masochism: Coldness and Cruelty*. New York: Zone Books.

Deleyto, Celestino (1997) 'The Margins of Pleasure: Female Monstrosity and Male Paranoia in *Basic Instinct*', *Film Criticism*, 21, 3, 20–43.

Derry, Charles (1988) *The Suspense Thriller: Films in the Shadow of Alfred Hitchcock.*
Jefferson, NC: McFarland.
Doane, Mary Ann (1987) *The Desire to Desire: The Woman's Film of the 1940s.*
Bloomington: Indiana University Press.
____ (1988) '*Caught* and *Rebecca*', in Constance Penley (ed.) *Feminism and Film Theory.*
New York: Routledge, 196–215.
____ (1991) *Femmes Fatales: Feminism, Film Theory, Psychoanalysis.* New York and
London: Routledge.
____ (1999 [1982]) 'Film and Masquerade: Theorising the Female Spectator', in Sue
Thornham (ed.) *Feminist Film Theory: A Reader.* Edinburgh: Edinburgh University
Press, 131–56.
Doane, Mary Ann and Janet Bergstrom (eds) (1989) *Camera Obscura*, 'The Spectatrix'
special issue.
Dyer, Richard (ed.) (1981) *Coronation Street.* London: British Film Institute.
____ (1982) 'Don't Look Now – The Male Pin-Up', *Screen*, 23, 3–4, 61–73.
____ (1986) 'Entertainment as Utopia', in Rick Altman (ed.) *Genre: The Musical.* London:
British Film Institute, 175–89.
Easthope, Anthony (1993) 'Introduction', in Anthony Easthope (ed.) *Contemporary Film
Theory.* London and New York: Longman, 1–26.
Erickson, Todd (1996) 'Kill Me Again: Movement becomes Genre', in Alain Silver and
James Ursini (eds) *Film Noir Reader.* New York: Limelight Editions, 307–30.
Feuer, Jane (1986) 'The Self-reflective Musical and the Myth of Entertainment', in Rick
Altman (ed.) *Genre: The Musical.* London: British Film Institute, 159–74.
Fischer, Lucy (1990) 'Seduced and Abandoned: Recollection and Romance in *Letter
from an Unknown Woman*', in Patricia Erens (ed.) *Issues in Feminist Film Criticism.*
Bloomington: Indiana University Press, 163–82.
Fischer, Lucy and Marcia Landy (1987) '*The Eyes of Laura Mars*: A Binocular Critique', in
Gregory A. Walker (ed.) *American Horrors: Essays on the Modern American Horror
Film.* Urbana: University of Illinois Press.
Fish, Stanley (1980) *Is There a Text in This Class?: The Authority of Interpretive
Communities.* Cambridge, MA: Harvard University Press.
Fitzpatrick Hanly, Margaret Ann (1995) 'Introduction to Masochism and Female
Psychology', in Margaret Ann Fitzpatrick Hanly (ed.) *Essential Papers on Masochism.*
New York: New York University Press, 405–10.
Freud, Sigmund (1991a [1920]) 'Beyond the Pleasure Principle', in *On Metapsychology:
The Theory of Psychoanalysis.* Penguin Freud Library, 11, trans. James Strachey, ed.
Angela Richards. London: Penguin, 275–338.
____ (1991b [1924]) 'The Economic Problem of Masochism', in *On Metapsychology:
The Theory of Psychoanalysis.* Penguin Freud Library. 11, trans. James Strachey, ed.
Angela Richards. London: Penguin, 413–25.
____ (1991c [1933]) 'Femininity', in *New Introductory Lectures.* Penguin Freud Library. 2,
trans. James Strachey, eds James Strachey and Angela Richards. London: Penguin,
145–69.
____ (1991d [1927]) 'Fetishism', in *On Sexuality.* Penguin Freud Library, 7, trans. James

Strachey, ed. Angela Richards. London: Penguin, 351–57.

_____ (1993 [1919]) 'A Child is Being Beaten', in *On Psychopathology*. Penguin Freud Library. 10, trans. James Strachey, ed. Angela Richards. London: Penguin, 163–93.

Gaines, Jane (1990 [1984]) 'Women and Representation: Can We Enjoy Alternative Pleasure?', in Patricia Erens (ed.) *Issues in Feminist Film Criticism*. Blooming-ton: Indiana University Press, 75–92.

Gaut, Berys (2003) 'Naked Film: Dogme and its Limits', in Mette Hjört and Scott MacKenzie (eds) *Purity and Provocation: Dogme 95*. London: British Film Institute, 89–101.

Geraghty, Christine (1991) *Women and Soap Opera: A Study of Prime-Time Soaps*. Cambridge: Polity Press.

Gledhill, Christine (1988) 'Pleasurable Negotiations', in E. Deidre Pribram (ed.) *Female Spectators: Looking at Film and Television*. London: Verso, 64–89.

Guneratne, Anthony and Wimal Dissanayake (eds) (2003) *Rethinking Third Cinema*. New York: Routledge.

Gunning, Tom (1989) 'The Cinema of Attractions: Early Film, Its Spectator and the Avant-Garde', in Thomas Elsaesser and Adam Barker (eds) *Early Film*. London: British Film Institute, 56–62.

Hall, Stuart (1980 [1973]): 'Encoding/decoding', in Centre for Contemporary Cultural Studies (ed.) *Culture, Media, Language: Working Papers in Cultural Studies, 1972–79*. London: Hutchinson, 128–38.

Hansen, Miriam (1986) 'Pleasure, Ambivalence, Identification: Valentino and Female Spectatorship', *Cinema Journal*, 25, 4, 6–32.

_____ (1991) *Babel & Babylon: Spectatorship in American Silent Film*. Cambridge, MA: Harvard University Press.

Hart, Lynda (1994) *Fatal Women: Lesbian Sexuality and the Mark of Aggression*. Prince-ton, NJ: Princeton University Press.

_____ (1998) *Between the Body and the Flesh: Performing Sadomasochism*. New York: Columbia University Press.

Harvey, Sylvia (1980) *May' 68 and Film Culture*. London: British Film Institute.

Haskell, Molly (1974) *From Reverence to Rape*. Baltimore: Penguin.

Heath, Stephen (1974) 'Lessons from Brecht', *Screen*, 15, 2, 103–28.

_____ (1986 [1976]) 'Narrative Space', in Philip Rosen (ed.) *Narrative, Apparatus, Ideology: A Film Theory Reader*. New York: Columbia University Press, 379–420.

Hedges, Inez (1991) *Breaking the Frame: Film Language and the Experience of Limits*. Bloomington: Indiana University Press.

Helmore, Edward (2003) 'Frankly, We Prefer Sex with Clothes On', *The Observer*, 15 June. On-line. Available HTTP: http//observer.guardian.co.uk/international/story/0,6903,977766,00.html. (25 August 2005)

Hietala, Veijo (1991) *Situating the Subject in Film Theory: Meaning and Spectator-ship in Cinema*. Turun yliopisto: Turku.

Hoberman, J. (1998) 'Head Trips', *Village Voice*, 17 March, 59.

Hobson, Dorothy (1982) *Crossroads – The Drama of a Soap*. London: Methuen.

Holland, Norman N. (1980) 'Unity Identity Text Self', in Jane P. Thompkins (ed.)

Reader-Response Criticism: From Formalism to Post-Structuralism. Baltimore: Johns Hopkins University Press, 118–35.

Hunt, Leon (1993) 'What are Big Boys Made of? *Spartacus, El Cid* and the Male Epic', in Pat Kirkham and Janet Thumin (eds) *You Tarzan: Masculinity, Movies and Men*. London: Lawrence and Wishart, 65–83.

Iser, Wolfgang (1974) *The Implied Reader: Patterns of Communication in Prose Fiction from Bunyan to Beckett*. Baltimore: The Johns Hopkins University Press.

Johnston, Claire (1991 [1973]) 'Women's Cinema as Counter Cinema', in Claire Johnston (ed.) *Notes on Women's Cinema Screen Pamphlet 2*, Society for Education in Film and Television, Glasgow: Screen Reprint, 24–31.

_____ (1992 [1980]) 'The Social Subject', in *The Sexual Subject: A Screen Reader in Sexuality*. London: Routledge, 295–300.

Kaplan, E. Ann (1995) 'Film and History: Spectatorship, Transference, and Race', in Ralph Cohen and Michael Roth (eds) *History and...: Histories Within the Human Sciences*. Charlottesville, VA: Virginia University Press, 179–208.

Kelly, Richard (2000) *The Name of this Book is Dogme 95*. London: Faber and Faber.

Kerekes, David and David Slater (1994) *Killing For Culture: An Illustrated History of Death Film*. London: Creation Books.

King, Geoff (2005) *The Spectacle of the Real: From Hollywood to Reality TV and Beyond*. Bristol: Intellect.

Krutnik, Frank (1991) *In a Lonely Street: Men, Masculinity and Film Noir*. London: Routledge.

Krzywinska, Tanya (1996) *Sex and the Cinema*. London: Wallflower Press.

Kuhn, Annette (1992 [1984]) 'Women's Genres', in *The Sexual Subject: A Screen Reader in Sexuality*. London: Routledge, 301–11.

_____ (1994) *Women's Pictures: Feminism and Cinema*. London: Verso.

Laplanche, Jean (1976) *Life and Death in Psychoanalysis*. Trans. Jeffrey Mehlman. Baltimore: The Johns Hopkins University Press.

Lapsley, Robert and Michael Westlake (1989) *Film Theory: An Introduction*. Man-chester: Manchester University Press.

Lermer, Richard (1991), 'Grace Jones Unzipped [interview with Grace Jones]', *The Advocate*, 10 September, 75.

'Lesbians and Gay Men in the U.S. Military: Historical Background', On-Line. Available HTTP: http://psychology.ucdavis.edu/rainbow/html/military_history.html (12 Oct. 2005).

Levinas, Emmanuel (1969) *Totality and Infinity: An Essay on Exteriority*, trans. Alphonso Lingis. Pittsburgh: Duquesne University Press.

_____ (1981) *Otherwise than Being or Beyond Essence*, trans. Alphonso Lingis. Boston: Martinus Nijhoff.

_____ (1989) 'Ethics as First Philosophy', in Sean Hand (ed.) *The Levinas Reader*. Cambridge, MA: Blackwell, 75–87.

Loewenstein, Rudolph M. (1995) 'A Contribution to the Psychoanalytic Theory of Masochism', in Margaret Ann Fitzpatrick Hanly (ed.) *Essential Papers on Masochism*. New York: New York University Press, 35–61.

Lopez, Robert and Jeff Marx (2003) 'The Internet is for Porn', *Avenue Q: Original Broadway Cast Recording*. New York: RCA Victor.

Lowenstein, Adam (2000) '"Under-the-skin Horrors": Social Realism and Classlessness in *Peeping Tom* and the British New Wave', in Justine Ashby and Andrew Higson (eds) *British Cinema, Past and Present*. London: Routledge, 221–32.

Maltby, Richard (1995) *Hollywood Cinema*. Malden, MA: Blackwell.

Mansfield, Nick (1997) *Masochism: The Art of Power*. Westport, CT: Praeger.

Massé, Michelle A. (1992) *In the Name of Love: Women, Masochism, and the Gothic*. Ithaca: Cornell University Press.

Mayne, Judith (1993) *Cinema and Spectatorship*. London and New York: Rouledge.

MacKinnon, Kenneth (1999) 'After Mulvey: Male Erotic Objectification', in Michele Aaron (ed.) *The Body's Perilous Pleasures: Dangerous Desires and Contemporary Culture*. Edinburgh: Edinburgh University Press, 13–29.

Metz, Christian (1982 [1975]) *The Imaginary Signifier: Psychoanalysis and the Cinema*, trans. Celia Britton, Annwyl Williams, Ben Brewster and Alfred Guzzetti. Bloomington: Indiana University Press.

____ (1985 [1974]) 'Story Discourse: A Note on Two Kinds of Voyeurism', in Bill Nichols (ed.) *Movies and Methods Volume II: An Anthology*. Berkeley, CA: University of California Press, 543–9.

Miller, Jacques-Alain (1977/78) 'Suture, Elements of the Logic of the Signifier', in 'Dossier on Suture', *Screen*, 18, 4, 24–34.

Mizejewski, Linda (1992) *Divine Decadence: Fascism, Female Spectacle and the Makings of Sally Bowles*. Princeton, NJ: Princeton University Press.

Modleski, Tania (1988) *The Women Who Knew Too Much: Hitchcock and Feminist Theory*. London: Routledge.

Moretti, Franco (1983) *Signs Taken for Wonders*, trans. Susan Fischer, David Forgacs and David Miller. London: Verso.

Morley, David (1980) *The 'Nationwide' Audience: Structure and Decoding*. London: British Film Institute.

____ (1983) 'Cultural Transformations: The Politics of Resistance', in Howard Davis and Paul Walton (eds) *Language, Image, Media*. Oxford: Basil Blackwell, 104–17.

Mulvey, Laura (1992 [1975]) 'Visual Pleasure and Narrative Cinema', in *The Sexual Subject: A Screen Reader in Sexuality*. London: Routledge, 22–34.

____ (1989 [1981]) 'Afterthoughts on "Visual Pleasure and Narrative Cinema" inspired by *Duel in the Sun*', in *Visual and Other Pleasures*. London: Macmillan, 29–38.

____ (2005) 'Death 24 X A Second: Stillness and the Moving Image', School of Drama, Film and Visual Arts Research Seminar, University of Kent.

Myers, James (1992) 'Nonmainstream Body Modification: Genital Piercing, Branding, Burning, and Cutting', *Journal of Contemporary Ethnography*, 21, 3, 267–306.

Neale, Steve (1993 [1983]) 'Masculinity as Spectacle: Reflections on Men and Mainstream Cinema', in Steven Cohan and Ina Rae Hark (eds) *Screening the Male: Exploring Masculinities in Hollywood Cinema*. London: Routledge, 9–20.

Noyes, John K. (1997) *The Mastery of Submission: Inventions of Masochism*. Ithaca: Cornell University Press.

Oudart, Jean-Pierre (1990) 'Cinema and Suture', in *Cahiers du cinéma 1969–1972: The Politics of Representation*. London: Routledge, 45–57.

Patton, Cindy (1989) 'Hegemony and Orgasm – or the Instability of Heterosexual Pornography', *Screen*, 30, 2, 100–12.

Pearl, Monica B. (1999) 'Symptoms of AIDS in Contemporary Film: Mortal Anxiety in an Age of Sexual Panic', in Michele Aaron (ed.) *The Body's Perilous Pleasures: Dangerous Desires and Contemporary Culture*. Edinburgh: Edinburgh University Press, 210–25.

_____ (2004) 'AIDS and New Queer Cinema', in Michele Aaron (ed.) *New Queer Cinema: A Critical Reader*. Edinburgh: Edinburgh University Press, 23–35.

Phillips, Anita (1998) *A Defence of Masochism*. London: Faber and Faber.

Plantinga, Carl and Greg M. Smith (eds) (1999) *Passionate Views: Film, Cognition and Emotion*. Baltimore: Johns Hopkins University Press.

Pleynet, Marcel (1969) 'Interview [with Gerard Leblanc]', *Cinéthique*, 3.

Poulet, George (1969) 'Phenomenology of Reading', *New Literary History*, 1, 53–68.

Rascaroli, Laura (1998) 'Strange Visions: Kathryn Bigelow's Metafiction', *Enculturation*, 2, 1, On-line. Available: HTTP http:www:enculturation (accessed 11 July 2005).

Reader, Keith A. (1993) *The May 1968 Events in France: Reproductions and Inter-pretations*. London: St. Martin's Press.

Reik, Theodor (1941) *Masochism in Modern Man*, trans. Margaret H. Beigel and Gertrud M. Kurth. New York: Grove Press.

Rich, B. Ruby (1990 [1978]) 'In the Name of Feminist Film Criticism', in Patricia Erens (ed.) *Issues in Feminist Film Criticism*. Bloomington: Indiana University Press, 268–87.

Riviere, John (1991 [1929]) 'Womanliness as a Masquerade', in Athol Hughes (ed.) *The Inner World and Joan Riviere: Collected Papers 1920–1958*. London: Karnac Books, 90–101.

Rodowick, D. N. (1991) *The Difficulty of Difference: Psychoanalysis, Sexual Diff-erence, and Film Theory*. New York: Routledge.

Rosen, Philip (ed.) (1986) *Narrative, Apparatus, Ideology: A Film Theory Reader*. New York: Columbia University Press.

Savran, David (1998) *Taking It Like a Man: White Masculinity, Masochism, and Con-temporary American Culture*. Princeton: Princeton University Press.

Scott, Graham G. (1983) *Erotic Power: An Exploration of Dominance and Submission*. New York: Citadel.

Shaviro, Steven (1993) *The Cinematic Body*. Minneapolis: University of Minnesota.

Shwartz, Vanessa R. (1995) 'Cinematic Spectatorship before the Apparatus: The Public Taste for Reality in *Fin-de-Siècle* Paris', in Leo Charney and Vanessa R. Shwartz (eds) *Cinema and the Invention of Modern Life*. Berkeley, CA: University of California Press, 297–319.

Siegel, Carol (1995) *Male Masochism: Modern Revisions of the Story of Love*. Bloom-ington: Indiana University Press.

Silver, Alain (1996) 'Son of Noir: Neo-Film Noir and the Neo-B Picture', in Alain Silver & James Ursini (eds) *Film Noir Reader*. New York: Limelight Editions, 331–38.

Silver, Alain and James Ursini (eds) (1996) *Film Noir Reader*. New York: Limelight Editions.

Silverman, Kaja (1983) *The Subject of Semiotics*. New York: Oxford University Press.

____ (1988) *The Acoustic Mirror: The Female Voice in Psychoanalysis and Cinema*. Bloomington: Indiana University Press.

____ (1992) *Male Subjectivity at the Margins*. New York: Routledge.

Simpson, Mark (1994a) *Male Impersonators: Men Performing Masculinity*. London: Routledge.

____ (1994b) 'Here come the mirror men', *Independent*, London, 15 November, 22.

Slack, Jennifer Daryl and Laurie Anne Whitt (1992) 'Ethics and Cultural Studies', in Lawrence Grossberg, Cary Nelson and Paula A. Treichler (eds) *Cultural Studies*. New York and London: Routledge, 571–92.

Smelik, Anneke (1999) 'Feminist Film theory', in Pam Cook and Mieke Bernink (eds) *The Cinema Book*, second edition. London: British Film Institute, 353–63.

Smirnoff, Victor N. (1995) 'The Masochistic Contract', in Margaret Ann Fitzpatrick Hanly (ed.) *Essential Papers on Masochism*. New York: New York University Press, 62–73.

Smith, Murray (1995) *Engaging Characters: Fiction, Emotion, and the Cinema*. Oxford: Oxford University Press.

Sontag, Susan (1997) *On Photography*. New York: Dell.

____ (2003) *Regarding the Pain of Others*. London: Hamish Hamilton.

Stacey, Jackie (1992 [1987]) 'Desperately Seeking Difference', in *The Sexual Subject: A Screen Reader in Sexuality*. London: Routledge, 244–57.

____ (1994) *Star Gazing: Hollywood Cinema and Female Spectatorship*. London: Routledge.

____ (1997) *Teratologies: A Cultural Study of Cancer*. London: Routledge.

Staiger, Janet (1992) *Interpreting Films: Studies in the Historical Reception of American Cinema*. Princeton, NJ: Princeton University Press.

____ (2000) *Perverse Spectators: The Practices of Film Reception*. New York: New York University Press.

Stevenson, Jack (2003) *Dogme Uncut: Lars von Trier, Thomas Winterberg, and the Gang that Took on Hollywood*. Santa Monica, CA: Santa Monica Press.

Stewart, Suzanne R. (1998) *Sublime Surrender: Male Masochism at the Fin-de-siecle*. Ithaca: Cornell University Press.

Stokes, Melvyn and Richard Maltby (2001) 'Introduction', in Melvyn Stokes and Richard Maltby (eds) *Hollywood Spectatorship: Changing Perceptions of Cinema Audiences*. London: British Film Institute, 1–22.

Studlar, Gaylyn (1985) 'Masochism and the Perverse Pleasures of Cinema', in Bill Nichols, *Movies and Methods Volume II: An Anthology*. Berkeley, CA: University of California Press, 602–21.

____ (1988) *In the Realm of Pleasure: Von Sternberg, Dietrich, and the Masochistic Aesthetic*. New York: Columbia University Press.

____ (1994) 'Masochistic Performance and Female Subjectivity in *Letter from an Unknown Woman*', in *Cinema Journal*, 33, 3, 35–57.

Sutton, Paul (1999) 'Cinematic Spectatorship as Procrastinatory Practice', *Parallax*, 5, 1, 80–2.

Sweetman, Paul (1999) 'Only Skin Deep? Tattooing, Piercing and the Transgressive Body', in Michele Aaron (ed.) *The Body's Perilous Pleasures: Dangerous Desires and Contemporary Culture*. Edinburgh: Edinburgh University Press, 165–87.

Thompson, Bill (1994) *Sadomasochism: Painful Perversion or Pleasurable Play?* London: Cassell.

Tuska, Jon (1984) *Dark Cinema: American Film Noir in Cultural Perspective*. Westport, CT: Greenwood Press.

Vallier, Claire and Ronnie Lippens (2004) 'Moving Images, Ethics and Justice', in *Punishment & Society*, 6, 3, 319–33.

Walden, Elizabeth (2002) 'Cultural Studies and the Ethics of Everyday Life', in *Culture Machine*, 4, The Ethico-Political Issue. On-line. Available HTTP: http://culturemachine.tees.ac.uk (acccessed 14 March 2005).

Wallace, Lee (2000) 'Continuous Sex: the Editing of Homosexuality in *Bound* and *Rope*', *Screen*, 41, 4, 369–87.

White, Patricia (1999) *Uninvited: Classical Hollywood Cinema and Lesbian Representability*. Bloomington: Indiana University Press.

Willemen, Paul (1981) 'Anthony Mann: Looking at the Male', *Framework*, 15/16/17, 16–20.

Williams, Linda (1989) *Hard Core: Power, Pleasure and the 'Frenzy of the Visible'*. Berkeley: University of California Press.

____ (1990 [1984]) '"Something Else Besides a Mother": *Stella Dallas* and the Maternal Melodrama', in Patricia Erens (ed.) *Issues in Feminist Film Criticism*. Bloomington: Indiana University Press, 137–62.

____ (ed.) (1994) *Viewing Positions: Ways of Seeing Film*. New Brunswick, NJ: Rutgers University Press.

Williams, Linda Ruth (1989) 'Submission and Reading', *New Formations*, 7, 9–19.

____ (2004) 'No Sex Please We're American', *Sight and Sound*, 14, 1, 18–20.

____ (2005) *The Erotic Thriller in Contemporary Cinema*. Edinburgh: Edinburgh University Press.

Zylinska, Joanne (2005) *The Ethics of Cultural Studies*. London and New York: Continuum.

INDEX